Good Question!

Why Does Earth Spin?
AND OTHER QUESTIONS ABOUT . . .
Our Planet

STERLING CHILDREN'S BOOKS
New York

STERLING CHILDREN'S BOOKS
New York

An Imprint of Sterling Publishing
387 Park Avenue South
New York, NY 10016

Photo Credits: Alamy © RIA Novosti: 27; Getty Images © National Geographic Creative: 30; iStockphoto.com © IBorisoff: 15; © pjmorley: 22; © shaunl: 20; © t_kimura: 2, 3, 9, 10, 16, 21, 24, 26, 27, 31, 32; © teekid: 22, 26, 27, 30 (tape); © Akbar Nemati via sxc.hu: 26

ISBN 978-1-4549-0674-2 [hardcover]
ISBN 978-1-4549-0675-9 [paperback]

Library of Congress Cataloging-in-Publication Data

Carson, Mary Kay, author.
 Why does Earth spin? : and other questions about our planet / Mary Kay Carson.
   pages cm. -- (Good question)
Audience: K-3.
Includes bibliographical references and index.
 ISBN 978-1-4549-0675-9 (paperback) -- ISBN 978-1-4549-0674-2 (hardcover) 1. Earth (Planet)--Miscellanea--Juvenile literature. I. Title. II. Series: Good question!
 QB631.4.C378 2014
 525--dc23
                                                                                         2013019123

Distributed in Canada by Sterling Publishing
c/o Canadian Manda Group, 165 Dufferin Street
Toronto, Ontario, Canada M6K 3H6
Distributed in the United Kingdom by GMC Distribution Services
Castle Place, 166 High Street, Lewes, East Sussex, England BN7 1XU
Distributed in Australia by Capricorn Link (Australia) Pty. Ltd.
P.O. Box 704, Windsor, NSW 2756, Australia

Design by Andrea Miller
Paintings by Peter Bull

For information about custom editions, special sales, and premium and corporate purchases, please contact
Sterling Special Sales at 800-805-5489 or specialsales@sterlingpublishing.com.

Manufactured in China
Lot #:
2 4 6 8 10 9 7 5 3 1
10/13

www.sterlingpublishing.com/kids

CONTENTS

Where is planet Earth?

Each star in the night sky is a giant ball of hot, fiery gases. The sun is a star, too. Earth is a planet that circles around, or orbits, the sun. A planet is a huge sphere, or ball, that orbits a star. Planets and everything else that travels around a star—moons, asteroids, and comets—make up a solar system. Our solar system has the sun at its center. The sun is one of billions of stars in our galaxy, the Milky Way. The Milky Way is one of billions of galaxies in the universe.

Earth isn't the closest or farthest planet from the sun. It is not the biggest or smallest planet, either. Eight planets orbit the sun. Mercury, Venus, Earth, and Mars are the closest planets to the sun. They are all rocky, terrestrial planets, which means their surfaces are hard and solid. All four terrestrial planets, including Earth, have mountains, valleys, and volcanoes. The other four planets are made of gases and mushy liquids with no solid land. Jupiter, Saturn, Uranus, and Neptune are cold, gassy planets far from the sun. Earth is the third planet from the sun. It circles the sun between Venus and Mars. Venus is hotter than Earth, and Mars is colder. From space, Earth looks like a small blue marble because most of its surface is covered by water.

How big is Earth?

Earth is small for a planet. On Jupiter, there is a hurricane-like storm three times bigger than Earth! Earth is only the fifth largest planet in our solar system, but it is the biggest terrestrial planet. More than a dozen Mercury-sized planets could fit inside Earth. Venus is closest to Earth in size. The distance all the way around Earth's middle, its circumference, is about 24,900 miles, or 40,000 kilometers (40,000 km). Venus's circumference is about 1,250 miles (2,012 km) shorter. As a comparison, if Earth were the size of a basketball, Venus would be the size of a soccer ball.

Washington, DC
39° North Latitude
77° West Longitude

Prime Meridian

Equator

Where on Earth are you?

Earth may be a small planet, but it's a big place. The surface of Earth covers nearly 197 million square miles (510 million square kilometers). To make it easier to locate and describe specific places on Earth, we use a system of imaginary lines that form a grid.

Latitude lines go across and circle Earth. The most famous line of latitude is the equator, which wraps around Earth's middle. Lines of latitude start at 0 degrees (°) at the equator and go up to 90° north and down to 90° south. Lines of longitude run up and down between Earth's poles. The most famous line of longitude is the prime meridian. Longitude lines start at 0° at the prime meridian and then go 180° around west and 180° east. Any location can be described by a combination of longitude and latitude lines. The position of Washington, DC, is 39° N, 77° W. This means it is 39 degrees north of the equator and 77 degrees west of the prime meridian.

Earth is tiny compared to Jupiter, the largest planet in our solar system. But Earth is big compared to miniature Mercury.

Jupiter

Earth

Mercury

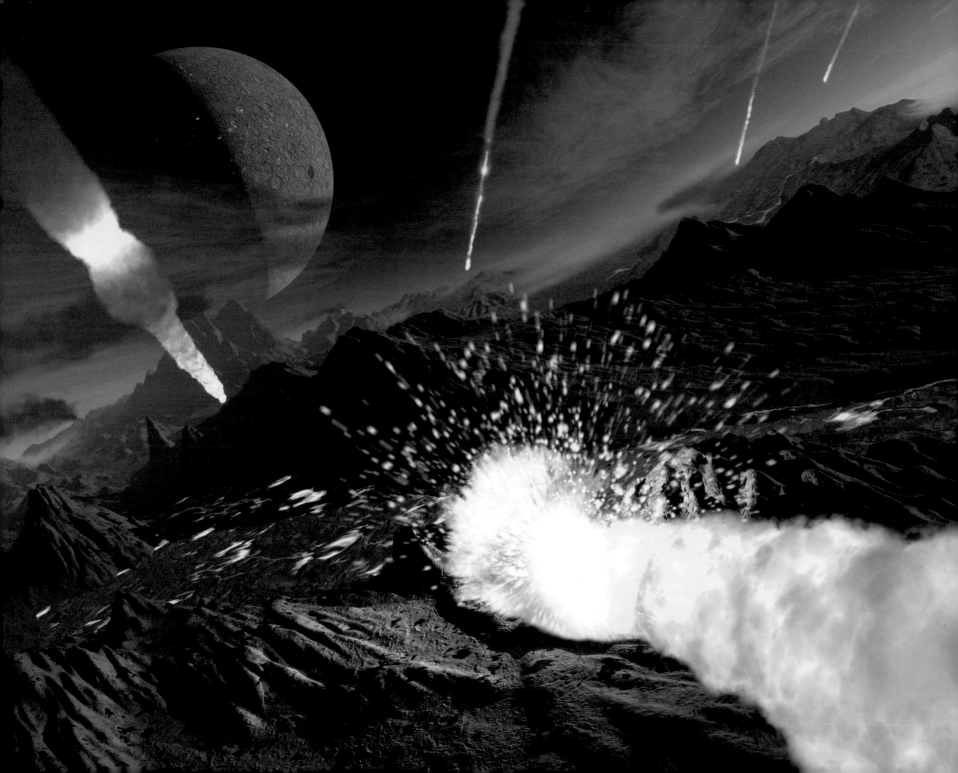

How old is our planet?

Our whole solar system, including Earth, formed from a cloud of dust and gas about 4½ billion years ago. That's a long time, but Earth has gone through a lot of changes over its history. Early Earth was a nightmarish place. Asteroids and comets from space pounded the planets. Those giant rocks were leftovers from the solar system's formation. They covered Earth and the moon with craters. On Earth, volcanoes across the planet spewed out seas of lava that melted and re-formed the land again and again. Volcanic eruptions released lots of toxic gases. Because of the asteroids falling from the sky, the high temperatures, and the poisonous gases, humans could not have survived on Earth when it was a young planet. After billions of years, plants and simple life-forms created enough oxygen to change Earth's atmosphere. Only then did the planet become liveable for humans and other animals.

Why does Earth spin?

The solar system formed out of swirling gas, circling rocks, and spinning space dust and debris. Planets were formed when some of that spinning space material clumped together into balls. The new planets continued to spin as they were formed and never stopped spinning. A planet spins around an imaginary line through its center called an axis. Every 24 hours our planet completes one spin on its axis. For some of those hours Earth is facing the sun. As our planet keeps turning, the sun sets where you are and day turns to night.

If Earth is spinning, why don't we feel like we're on an amusement park ride? Because everything else on Earth is moving, too. You don't feel the speed any more than you do while riding in a car. The cookie you're eating in a car that's moving at 60 miles per hour (97 kilometers per hour) doesn't seem like it is moving. Why not? Because everything else—your hand, mouth, and car seat—is moving at 60 miles per hour, too.

What is Earth made of?

As Earth was forming, it heated up and its insides melted. Heavy materials in the melted rock sank toward Earth's center. Lighter materials floated up to the top. This created layers inside Earth that still exist.

If you drilled down about 3,960 miles (6,370 km), you'd reach the very center of Earth. This is Earth's core, a ball of mostly iron and nickel. The metals are so squashed by the weight of the planet above them that they are squeezed into a solid inner core. Temperatures here range from 8,000 degrees Fahrenheit (8,000°F) to 12,000°F, or 4,450 degrees Celsius (4,450°C) to 6,650°C. Surrounding the solid inner core is the outer core. It is also made of metals, but they are less solid and more like a liquid. The next layer is the mantle. More than half of all the material making up Earth is in its middle mantle layer. The deepest part of the mantle is about 1,800 miles (2,900 km) below the surface. The mantle is a vast layer of hot, mushy melted rock that's moving.

The top layer is what you stand on, the crust. Compared with the mantle, it's an astonishingly thin layer, like an egg's shell or the skin of an apple. Earth's crust is thicker under land and thinner under the oceans. The rocks and minerals that make up the ocean floor and dry land are part of the crust. The crust of the continents is ten times older than the ocean crust. Scientists have found rocks in Australia that are 4 billion years old.

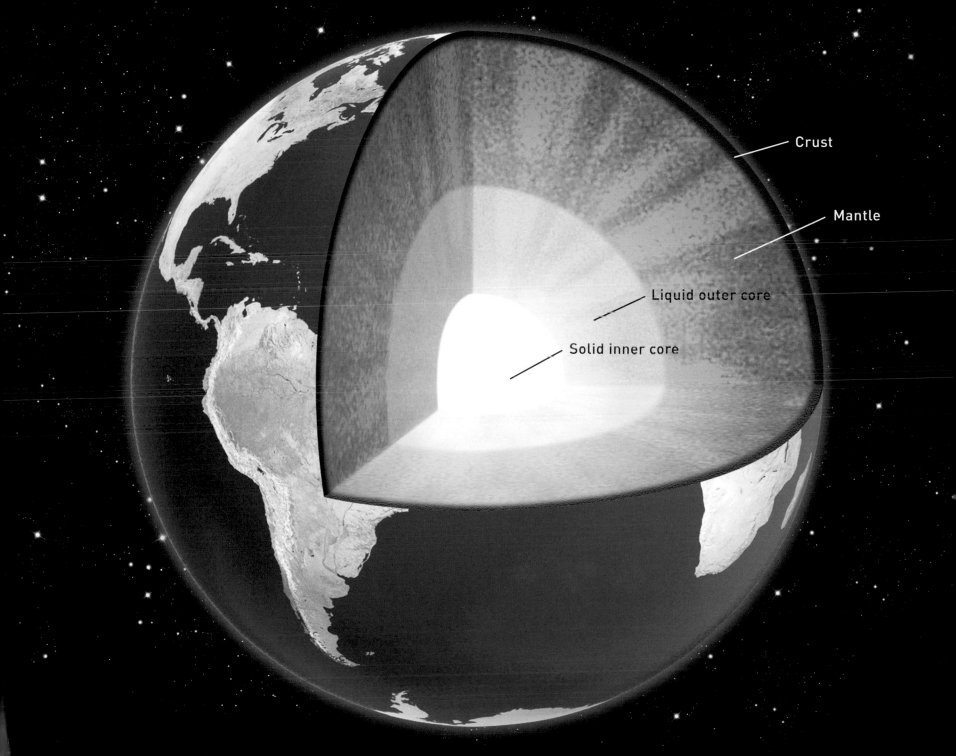

Crust

Mantle

Liquid outer core

Solid inner core

Mountains are made by clashing tectonic plates. As plates shove into each other and up and over one another, rock is pushed up into a growing mountain range.

Crust

Mountain range

Tectonic plate

Mantle

Tectonic plate

Does Earth move under our feet?

Earth's thin rocky crust is not connected to the layer below it. The crust just floats on top of the mantle, like crackers float on soup. The mushy rock of the mantle sinks down and rises up in slow flowing waves. The mantle's constant churning moves the crust floating on top of it, too. It breaks up the crust into big chunks. Earth's crust is broken up into about a dozen big pieces called tectonic plates. They fit together like puzzle pieces.

The ever-moving mantle scoots and drags the tectonic plates around the planet. Some of the faster plates move as much as 6 inches (15 centimeters) a year. Whatever is on top of the tectonic plates goes along with it. This is why the continents have changed their shape and position. About 250 million years ago, there was only a single continent, Pangea. It was a giant supercontinent. Over time, the moving tectonic plates broke up Pangea into today's seven continents—Antarctica, North America, South America, Africa, Australia, Asia, and Europe. In another 250 million years the continents will have drifted far enough to end up together again!

Clashing tectonic plates make for lots of action. Earthquakes, volcanoes, tsunamis, mountain-making, and seafloor spreading all happen where plates clash. It's the way Earth recycles its crust, makes new rocks, and changes its surface.

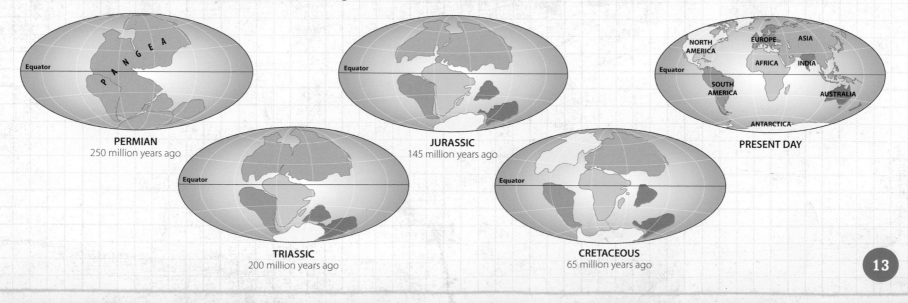

PERMIAN
250 million years ago

TRIASSIC
200 million years ago

JURASSIC
145 million years ago

CRETACEOUS
65 million years ago

PRESENT DAY

13

How much of our planet is covered in water?

Earth is an ocean planet. Seawater at least 2½ miles (4 km) deep covers 70 percent of Earth's surface. If Earth's surface were cut into ten even chunks, seven would be ocean. Mountains, forests, volcanoes, deserts, jungles, lakes, and rivers make up the other 30 percent of Earth's surface. Most of Earth's water is salty seawater. If all the water in the oceans disappeared, the layer of salt left behind would be as thick as half a football field. Freshwater is rare. If all Earth's water fit into a gallon jug, only about one-half cup of it would be freshwater.

Water is amazing stuff. It's the only natural substance that can exist as a liquid, a solid, and a gas at Earth's temperatures. Solid water, or ice, melts into liquid water on a sunny afternoon. Puddles of liquid water evaporate into water vapor, a gas. Water's special properties constantly change our planet. Water creates clouds and weather, breaks down rocks, and helps balance the planet's temperature.

Water also runs the chemistry of life. Plants and animals need water to live and grow. Water makes up much of our bodies. If you weigh 75 pounds, your body has enough water to fill about eleven large soda bottles. All life needs water. Life and water go together.

Oceans are home to nearly 50 percent
of all species on earth.

Why is there life on Earth?

Earth is the only place where life has been found. It is also the only planet with liquid water on its surface. Water is a big reason life is here. On our neighbor planet Venus, all water boiled away because that planet is so close to the sun. Earth's distance from the sun is just right for life. Our other neighbor, Mars, is colder because it is farther from the sun. Mars is also cold because of its very thin atmosphere. The blanket of gas around a planet is its atmosphere. Earth's atmosphere also helps makes life possible. It holds in heat and blocks out dangerous rays from the sun.

Life showed up early in Earth's history. It sprang up once life-supporting conditions were here—liquid water, mild temperatures, and a suitable atmosphere. Life has existed on Earth for at least the last 3.5 billion years. Early life changed Earth's atmosphere. It put more oxygen into the air. This made Earth able to support more kinds of life, including animals. Life continues to change our planet. Plants make oxygen and break up rocks. Today, life of some sort exists nearly everywhere on Earth—land, water, and air. Even boiling hot springs and frozen lakes are home to tiny life-forms. Scientists think there could be as many as 8.7 million different species, or kinds, of living things on Earth.

A thin layer of gases, the atmosphere, wraps around Earth. It gives us air to breathe and protects the planet from the sun's dangerous rays.

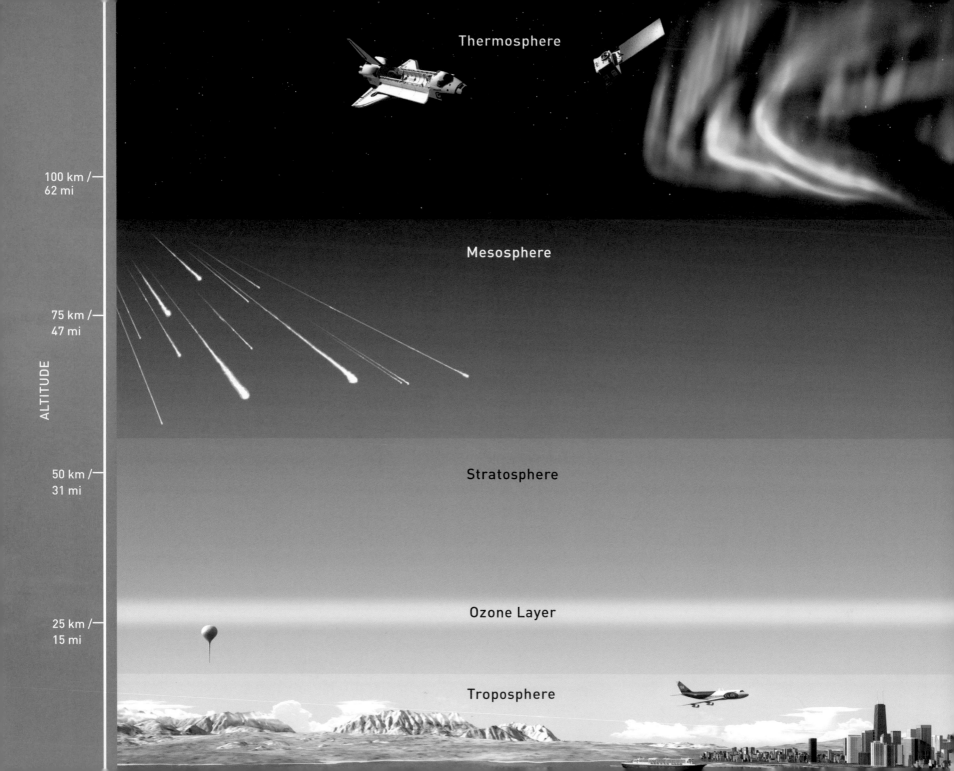

Thermosphere

Mesosphere

Stratosphere

Ozone Layer

Troposphere

ALTITUDE

100 km /
62 mi

75 km /
47 mi

50 km /
31 mi

25 km /
15 mi

Why is the sky blue?

Take a deep breath. You just breathed in some of Earth's atmosphere! The air between Earth's surface and outer space is called the atmosphere. Air is made up of different gases. Oxygen is the gas we need to power our bodies. But it is nitrogen gas that makes up more than three-fourths of our air. Nitrogen is also why the sky is blue. Sunlight bounces off nitrogen gas and scatters lots of blue light down toward us, so we see the sky as blue.

There is no blue sky out in space. Space starts about 60 miles (100 km) above Earth. There are still some gases beyond that, but not many. The atmosphere's gases are thickest at the surface but thin out the higher you go. You know this if you've ever climbed a mountain. There is less oxygen to breathe on mountaintops. Scientists divide the atmosphere into four main layers, from top to bottom. The layer nearest outer space is the thermosphere. This is where radio waves bounce around and colorful curtains of light called auroras ripple in bands of green, red, and blue. Below it is the mesosphere, where the air is not quite as thin. There are enough gases in the mesosphere to slow down and burn up meteors falling toward Earth. We see them as falling stars. The stratosphere is where the important ozone layer is. It protects us from dangerous solar rays. The lowest layer of the atmosphere is the troposphere. This is where breathable air is and where weather happens.

What creates our weather?

Earth's weather happens where the most air is. This is in the bottom layer of the atmosphere, the troposphere. The air here is always moving. The sun shines on the hills, oceans, and other surfaces of Earth. This heats up the air above them. Warm air is lighter than cold air, and so it rises. Warm air cools as it rises. The now cool air is heavy, and so it sinks back down. This constant up-and-down movement of air, driven by the sun, creates weather.

Weather is what is going on in the atmosphere at a specific place and time. Temperature is part of weather, and so is moving air, or wind. Water is the other basic weather ingredient besides air and sun. Earth's water is always moving between the surface and the air. Ocean water evaporates into the air and forms clouds that deliver rain and snow to faraway places. Clouds hold tons of water. A thunderstorm cloud holds as much water as what spills over Niagara Falls in six minutes. Weather helps move water from place to place.

Thunderstorm clouds grow into towering giants as warm, moist air rises inside them and adds more layers of dark, rain-filled clouds.

Why is the moon important to Earth?

Watching the moon change phases is a lot of fun. It goes from bright and full to a silvery sliver and back again. However, the moon is more than a lovely sight in the night sky. Earth would be a very different planet without it. The moon causes the water in oceans and large lakes to rise and fall each day—this is called the tide. The moon's pull on large bodies of water creates the tides. Tides go from low to high as the moon goes around Earth. The moon also keeps Earth from wobbling. Our moon helps lock in a steady orbit for our planet. This makes the seasons regular and the climate steady.

The moon can do all this because it's nearby and really big. It's large and heavy enough to affect Earth. How unusual is the moon? Lots of planets have moons. A moon is any space object that orbits a bigger space object. Giant Jupiter has more than sixty moons, and a few, such as Ganymede, are bigger than our moon. But our moon is quite large compared to the small size of Earth. Three of our moons lined up side by side would stretch nearly across Earth. It would take more than twenty-nine Ganymedes to stretch across Jupiter.

The moon is continually dragging ocean waters toward itself as it circles Earth every month. Daily tides happen as Earth spins on its axis and water is pulled toward the moon.

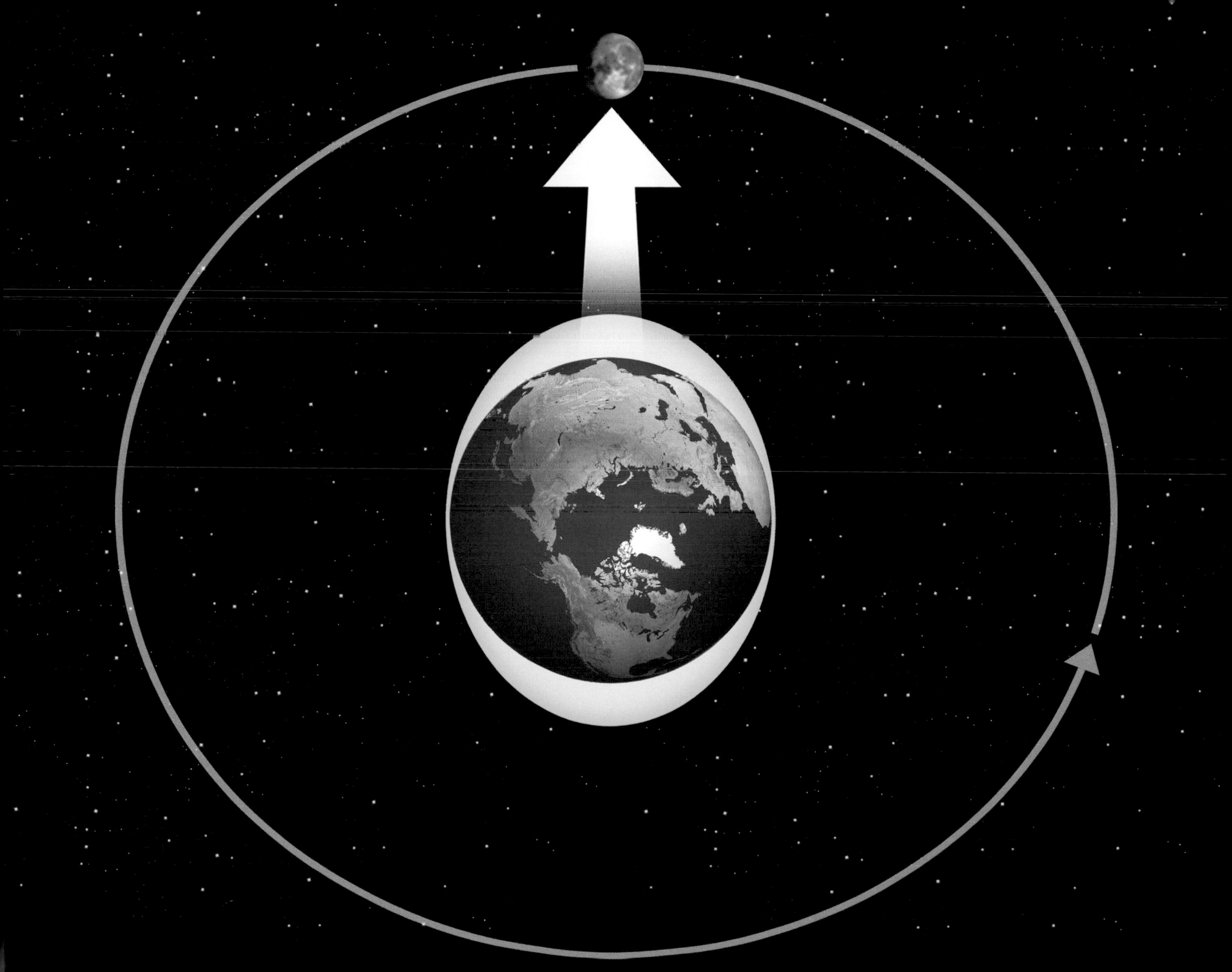

Why do we have seasons?

What time of year is it where you live? Is it summer or winter, spring or autumn? Earth, like the other planets, travels around the sun. The time it takes for Earth to make one orbit around the sun is one year. Why is part of the year warmer than other times? Because Earth is tilted. Earth's axis is not straight up and down—it's tilted. Imagine our planet as a ball of yarn with a knitting needle stuck through it. The ball of yarn would spin around with the knitting needle leaning a bit to the side.

Earth's tilted axis means that different parts of the planet get different amounts of sunlight. During part of Earth's orbit around the sun, the North Pole tips toward the sun. The top half of the planet gets more sunlight and has summer. Meanwhile, the bottom half of Earth tilts away from the sun, gets less sunlight, and has winter. Six months later Earth is on the other side of the sun. Then the South Pole tips toward the sun, and the bottom half of the planet gets more sunlight and has summer. Meanwhile, the top half has winter.

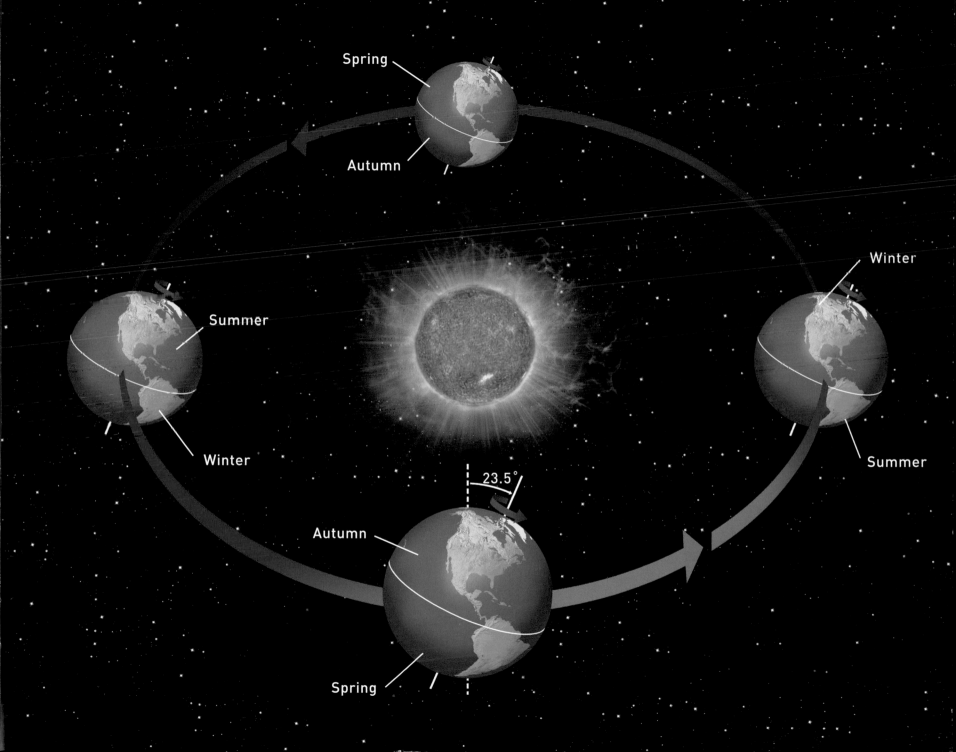

Spring

Autumn

Summer

Winter

Winter

Summer

23.5°

Autumn

Spring

Lut Desert is a large salt desert in southeastern Iran. It has some of the tallest sand dunes in the world.

What is the hottest place on Earth?

Deserts are the hottest places on the planet. A desert is a dry, bare place where it doesn't rain much, plants are few, and wildlife is limited. About a third of Earth's land is desert. All deserts are dry, but only some are hot. The hottest deserts are the ones that soak up the most sunlight. They are in countries near the equator where the directly overhead sun hits the land like a spotlight. Australia, North Africa, southern China, and Mexico have some of the hottest deserts. The very hottest? Lut Desert in Iran wins with a highest overall temperature of 159.3°F (70.7°C).

The Soviet Union founded Antarctica's Vostok Station in 1957. Today, scientists from all over the world do research there.

What is the coldest place on Earth?

O dd as it seems, the coldest spot on Earth is also a desert. Much of Antarctica gets very little snow and has few lakes or rivers, no plants, and few animals. The Vostok science station near the South Pole measured the record coldest temperature of –128.6°F (–89.2°C). Brrrr! What are the runners-up for the coldest location? The North Pole, Greenland, and Siberia can have temperatures as low as –90°F (–68°C). On a February day in Siberia, one weather scientist tossed boiling water from a cup into the air. It froze into snow before hitting the ground!

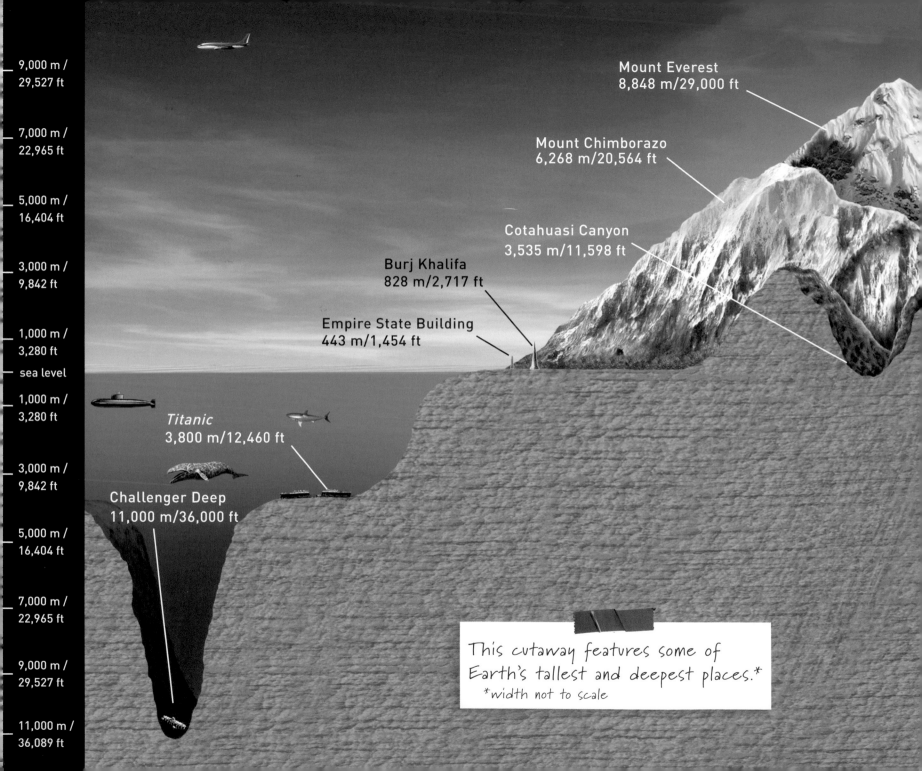

9,000 m /
29,527 ft

7,000 m /
22,965 ft

5,000 m /
16,404 ft

3,000 m /
9,842 ft

1,000 m /
3,280 ft

sea level

1,000 m /
3,280 ft

3,000 m /
9,842 ft

5,000 m /
16,404 ft

7,000 m /
22,965 ft

9,000 m /
29,527 ft

11,000 m /
36,089 ft

Mount Everest
8,848 m/29,000 ft

Mount Chimborazo
6,268 m/20,564 ft

Cotahuasi Canyon
3,535 m/11,598 ft

Burj Khalifa
828 m/2,717 ft

Empire State Building
443 m/1,454 ft

Titanic
3,800 m/12,460 ft

Challenger Deep
11,000 m/36,000 ft

This cutaway features some of
Earth's tallest and deepest places.*
*width not to scale

What is the highest place on Earth?

Mountains are the highest places on the planet. The tallest mountain is Mount Everest at more than 29,000 feet (8,848 meters) high. That's nearly up where jet airliners fly. As if it that wasn't tall enough, it's still growing! Mount Everest is part of the Himalayas Mountains. They are continually pushed up by the forces that created them—India's tectonic plate is pushing against the Eurasian Plate and shoving it higher and higher. The Himalayas continue to rise about an inch (2 cm) a year.

Mount Everest is the tallest mountain, but it is not the farthest from the center of Earth. A mountain In Ecuador, called Chimborazo, is that winner. How is that possible? Earth is not a perfectly round sphere. It is a bit fatter around its middle, like a slightly squashed orange. Although Everest is taller, Mount Chimborazo is 1½ miles (2.5 km) closer to outer space. Which do you think should be crowned "the highest"?

What is the deepest place on Earth?

When you think of deep places, canyons come to mind. Cotahuasi Canyon in southwestern Peru is Earth's deepest. It is more than 2 miles (about 3.5 km) down to its bottom. That's twice as deep as the Grand Canyon in Arizona.

There are deeper places in Earth's crust, however. Where? In the great deep itself—the ocean. The deepest part of the ocean is under the western Pacific Ocean halfway between Japan and New Guinea. Here lies Challenger Deep, a narrow slot-shaped canyon in the seafloor. At a depth of at least 6½ miles (11 km), it's the deepest place known. If Mount Everest were sunk down inside Challenger Deep, more than 1 mile (1.5 km) of ocean would cover its peak.

What does an Earth scientist study?

Earth scientists study Earth and its place in the universe. That covers a lot! Most Earth scientists concentrate on one subject. If you study rocks and minerals, you are a geologist. Geologists learn about Earth's history by looking at rocks. A geologist might look for oil or try to predict when a volcano will erupt. A type of Earth science that tries to predict the weather is meteorology. How do meteorologists see into the future? How do they know if it will be sunny or rainy? They take measurements of the atmosphere's temperature, winds, and gases. Meteorologists also track storms, predict where the danger will be, and send out weather warnings to communities.

Oceans are a huge part of our planet, and they have their own Earth science called oceanography. Oceanographers study all parts of the oceans—water, seafloor, and sea life. Believe it or not, part of Earth science is what's beyond Earth! Astronomers study stars, planets, moons, comets, and other space stuff. They are constantly learning more about how our small terrestrial ocean planet fits into the cosmos.

Earth scientists that study volcanoes are called volcanologists. This one is studying Mount Yasur on Tanna Island in the South Pacific.

FIND OUT MORE

Books to Read

Carson, Mary Kay. *Far-Out Guide to Earth*. Berkeley Heights,
    NJ: Enslow, 2010.
Ride, Sally, and Tam O'Shaughnessy. *Mission: Planet Earth: Our
    World and Its Climate — and How Humans Are Changing
    Them*. New York: Flash Point/Roaring Brook Press, 2009.
Snedden, Robert. *Mapping Earth from Space*. Chicago:
    Heinemann-Raintree, 2011.
Solway, Andrew. *Why Is There Life on Earth?* Chicago:
    Heinemann-Raintree, 2011.
Taylor, Barbara. *Navigators: Planet Earth*. New York:
    Kingfisher, 2012.
Turner, Pamela S. *Life on Earth—and Beyond: An
    Astrobiologist's Quest*. Watertown, MA: Charlesbridge,
    2008.

Websites to Visit

EARTH OBSERVATORY
http://earthobservatory.nasa.gov
    Check out amazing satellite pictures and maps of
    our planet.

EPA CLIMATE CHANGE KIDS SITE
http://epa.gov/climatechange/kids/
    Read and learn about climate change.

FOR KIDS ONLY: EARTH SCIENCE
http://kids.earth.nasa.gov/
    Learn about land, water, air, and natural hazards
    and play Earth science games, too.

INDEX

newbrow

CONTEMPORARY

CONTEMPORARY ARTISTS

50

SHANE POMAJAMBO

Schiffer Publishing Ltd

4880 Lower Valley Road • Atglen, PA 19310

Copyright © 2012 by Shane Pomajambo

Library of Congress Control Number: 2012933231

Designed by Justin Watkinson
Cover by Bruce Waters
Type set in Bauhaus BT/Gill Sans Std

ISBN: 978-0-7643-4056-7
Printed in China

Schiffer Books are available at special discounts for bulk purchases for sales promotions or premiums. Special editions, including personalized covers, corporate imprints, and excerpts can be created in large quantities for special needs. For more information contact the publisher:

Published by Schiffer Publishing Ltd.
4880 Lower Valley Road
Atglen, PA 19310
Phone: (610) 593-1777; Fax: (610) 593-2002
E-mail: Info@schifferbooks.com

For the largest selection of fine reference books on this and related subjects, please visit our website at
www.schifferbooks.com
We are always looking for people to write books on new and related subjects. If you have an idea for a book, please contact us at proposals@schifferbooks.com

This book may be purchased from the publisher.
Please try your bookstore first.
You may write for a free catalog.

In Europe, Schiffer books are distributed by:
Bushwood Books
6 Marksbury Ave.
Kew Gardens
Surrey TW9 4JF England
Phone: 44 (0) 20 8392 8585; Fax: 44 (0) 20 8392 9876
E-mail: info@bushwoodbooks.co.uk
Website: www.bushwoodbooks.co.uk

Art Whino is a Washington, DC-based art gallery whose mission is to bring together the pioneers and freshest talent from around the world. With more than 1,200 artists in the Art Whino arsenal, ranging from California to New York, Germany to Japan, and beyond, Art Whino has become an all-encompassing force in the art world. Exhibitions cover the whole spectrum of new art forms ranging from emerging artists working with stencil and wheat pasting to the most skilled leaders of the low brow movement. The artists in this book are either represented by Art Whino or have shown with us in the past.

To see more work from these artists please visit www.**Artwhino**.com

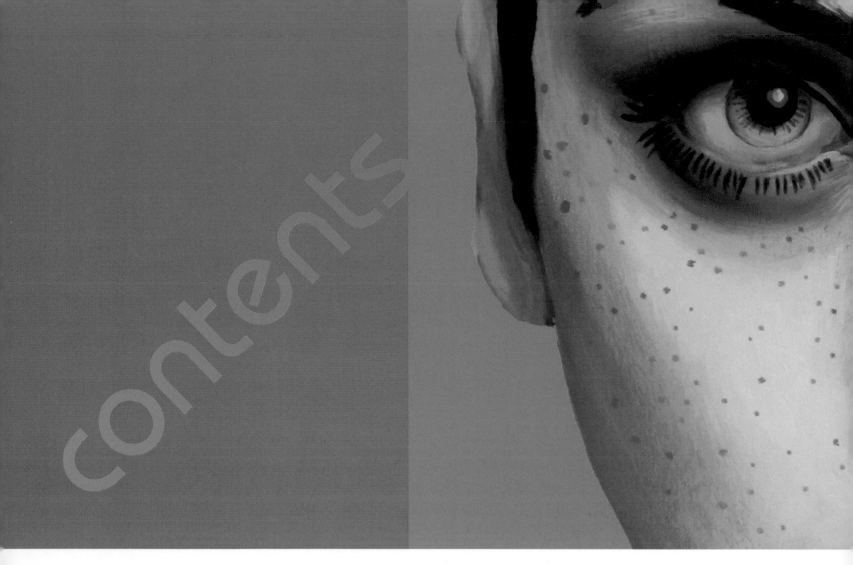

contents

artists' contact
information

If this is your first introduction to Art Whino and this art genre, you are probably wondering who I am and what this book is all about. To understand how this compilation of artists came to be, I feel it is important to start at the beginning, where I come from, why Art Whino opened its doors, and what this artwork is.

I grew up in Queens, New York, surrounded by the 1980s birth of rap, break dancing, and most importantly, graffiti. These new forms of expression were a new voice, a voice that I could identify with, that represented the place I came from. Train cars were the first canvas of this new art form. A battle raged between transit police buffing and arresting the "writers" and the writers risking their lives by hopping over fences and crossing over third rails to get a chance to do the next piece. This continued until transit police stepped up security, trains were switched to spray paint resistant stainless steel, and were cleaned before being sent out to carry the commuting public.

This was the turning point of graffiti. Writers switched gears and began bombin' walls, and so began the "Underground" world of street art. There was no avoiding it. Graffiti in New York was in your face and there to stay. Although the new art form was becoming as much a part of New York as the Statue of Liberty, the identities of writers went unknown and their work was only recognized by their evolving styles—after all, their work invaded public space and was considered vandalism.

Going into the '90s, the graffiti world continued to evolve as I grew further away from it. I was now living in the Washington, DC, area and in college. Six years of school and a master's degree later, I was immersed in the world of architecture and had lost touch with the subculture that I felt once represented me. It was no longer a part of my landscape. As life so often does though, fate found a way of taking me back.

I will never forget the single event that brought all these memories back. I ran across an article about Doze Green, part of Rock Steady Crew in the '80s, and a legendary graffiti writer. All at once I remembered how much I admired his character work and began to wonder what happened to the many other writers I had once been familiar with. I decided it was time to reconnect with this part of my past and was happily surprised to see that many of these writers were now recognized as artists and were showing their work in galleries. This piqued my curiosity and I began wondering what was going on in the contemporary art scene.

I began connecting the dots and was led all the way to California, where a new art movement was exploding onto the West Coast art scene, this one stemming from the skateboarding culture. Just as on the East Coast, this was a new genre, representative of its current culture and, once again, something I could relate to.

For the next few years I followed East and West Coast artists closely by signing up for gallery mailing lists as I continued my life as an architect in Washington, DC. The art world took a rising presence in my life with my growing knowledge of the art scene and my escalating collection of artwork, starting with prints and evolving into originals. I just couldn't get enough; I was addicted to art. I couldn't just let this be a New York and LA thing, I felt a responsibility to introduce DC to the artwork that I needed in my life. I started the gallery and named it Art Whino because I felt the name perfectly represented this irrepressible need for art.

So, what is this addictive art? For me it is a raw unapologetic form of expression that represents today's current culture. The artwork varies depending on the artist's roots and influences, but the need to represent the society we live in is unchanging. The work ranges from street artists who trace back to the '80s hip-hop culture, using tools such as stenciling, wheat pasting, spray paint, and guerilla art installations, to illustrative artists who trace their backgrounds to graphic design and illustration. The illustrative artists usually choose pop culture as their subject matter or create a surrealist world through a stylistic approach. Many of these artists further their work by dabbling in the world of custom collectibles and move from canvas to vinyl figures which they customized as 3D extensions of their work. A lot of the artists are self-taught and the majority of them do it for themselves. It's mostly this attitude towards their work that has the art world coining the phrase "Low Brow" art for the genre. This term began in the '70s and most artists have embraced it over alternatives such as "urban contemporary," which lumps too many styles into one box. Some, like Banksy, using the term "New Brow," are more recognized by the art community. Regardless what you call it, for me, this scene is just like the '80s hip-hop culture in the sense that it feels like a family. Like in any family, there are disagreements, but they are family nonetheless.

Since opening the gallery in 2007, I have been privileged to work with more than 1,200 artists. Although working styles and personalities may vary, the overall uniting quality has been the overwhelming amount of support and positivity I've been met with.

Choosing the fifty artists to feature here was no easy task. I chose this group, from all of these artists I so greatly admire, because they represent the wide array of work being created in this new movement. Not only do they stand for the many interpretations of Low Brow, they are also great supporters of the mission at Art Whino. Of course there are so many more artists that I wish I could have included, to which I have to say, there will be more books and soon enough your work will also be featured. Thank you to all the amazing artists that give purpose to this profession.

ART WHINO Gallery
120 American Way
National Harbor, MD 20745
(301) 567-8210

www.ArtWhino.com

www.Facebook/ArtWhino

www.flickr.com/ArtWhino

sts

Peter Adamyan

California

Peter Adamyan was born in 1987 in the suburbs of Los Angeles. Like most children from a single-parent household, his second parent was inevitably the television. He spent his youth in front of the TV with pencil and paper in hand, drawing his favorite cartoon characters and super heroes. In his teens Adamyan took art more seriously, taking as many high school art classes as he could and reading as many art books on techniques and mediums as he could stand. Mostly self taught, Adamyan has reverted back to his childhood roots, taking his inspiration from popular culture and using it to his advantage as a type of symbolism for the real message of his paintings. As his medium he has created a style that involves cut out pieces of wood, layered on top of one an other and rendered in a colorful realism.

Give Me Your Tired, Your Papayas, Your Hurting Gases Yearning to Be Frijoles, 2011. Oil and acrylic on wood relief, 13" x 13" (33 x 33 cm).

Painting to a Christian Nation (God Bless This Mess), 2010. Oil on wood relief, 33" x 44" (84 x 112 cm).

The Fat Ass Saves the Day as the Artist Contemplates the Fate of Coochy Cooty and America's Over Consumption of Non-Kosher Delicacies, 2009.
Oil on wood relief, 18" x 20" (46 x 51 cm).

Brett Amory
California

Brett Amory was born in 1975 in Chesapeake, Virginia. He lived in San Francisco for 15 years before relocating to Oakland in 2009, where he is currently based. His work has been shown in Los Angeles, San Francisco, London, New York, and San Jose, and continues to receive acclaim. Amory began the *Waiting* series in 2001 with paintings based on photographs the artist took of ordinary city architecture and random people who he saw daily but never spoke to. He feels especially drawn to individuals who look lost, lonely, or awkward—those who don't appear to fit in socially. As the title suggests, the *Waiting* series depicts how people are distracted by constant internal dialogue, preoccupied with memories of the past, and/or concerned for the future—never able to live in the present moment. Amory's work attempts to visually represent this concept of disconnection, detachment, and anticipation, conveying the idea of transient temporality that exists in the moments of our daily lives.

Waiting #83, 2011. Oil on panel, 42" x 60" (107 x 152 cm).

Waiting #78, 2011. Oil on panel, 48" x 72" (122 x 183 cm).

Waiting #81, 2011. Oil on panel, 24" x 48" (61 x 122 cm).

Morten Andersen
Denmark

There is something crisp and foreign in Morten's multidimensional pieces. Nothing stands still. The dynamics are almost endless. The futuristic shapes and figures mesh, overlap, and twist around each other. The elements, vacillating between sharply defined, transparent, and dissolving, breathe life into the motifs and make them ooze exuberance. Although Morten's inspiration and style encompass remnants from both Jorn and Kirkeby, with their intuitive shapes and explosions of color, and Ib Geertsen and Per Arnoldi's contrastingly tight geometric modes of expression, he is entirely his own person. His compositions are plainly innovative and he certainly belongs within the group of unschooled artists poised to have a break-through, effortlessly standing out. Respect for that.

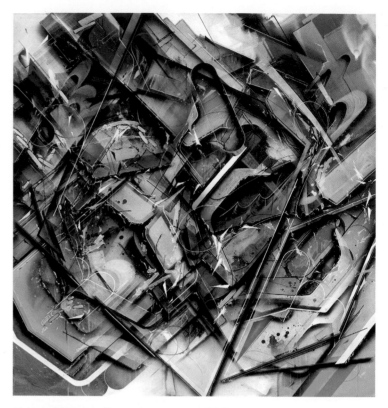

Nobody, 2011. Acrylic, markers, spray, and ink on canvas, 63" x 67" (160 x 170 cm).

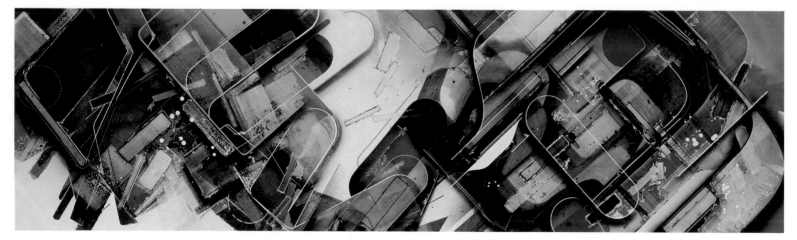

Milky Lopsided, 2011. Acrylic, markers, spray and ink on canvas, 24" x 83" (60 x 210 cm).

Robot Breath, 2011. Acrylics, markers, spray, and ink on canvas, 48" x 61" (123 x 156 cm).

Angry Woebots
California

Aaron Martin was born on the island Oahu, Hawaii, in 1977. Most of his childhood was spent growing up and moving from Southern California to Nevada before finally landing back in Hawaii during his junior year of high school. In 1999 a car accident changed everything; this life-threatening experience inspired him to leave the island once again, this time to Seattle, Washington. Inspired by the rain and being indoors, he started playing around with different art mediums again. He then went back to Hawaii with a new perspective. Aaron had his first show in 2002 and has not stopped. He has showed in galleries up and down California, the East Coast, and even in shows that have traveled from the U.S. to Hong Kong. His focal medium is acrylic paintings on wood and canvas. Using minimal colors and detailed character design, these paintings are usually comprised of stressed out emotional pandas. The pandas tend to represent the story of struggle.

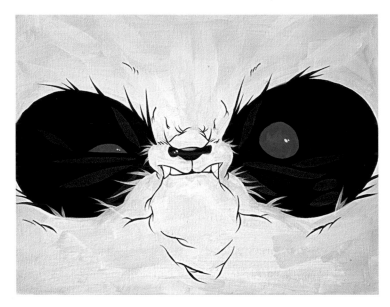

Smug, 2011. Acrylic on canvas, 16" x 11" (41 x 28 cm).

Mono Cali King. Resin sculpture, hand painted acrylic, 8" (20 cm).

Distance Makes the Heart Grow Monsters. Digital vector design.

War Paint, 2011. Acrylic on wood, 18" x 14" (46 x 36 cm).

Glenn Arthur

California

Glenn Arthur is a self-taught visual artist from Orange County, California. Born in February of 1979, he grew up in a conservative, religious household with little to no influence in art. After shedding his roots, he quickly realized that creating art would be his calling. Although he constantly doodled and sketched throughout his youth, Glenn did not come into painting until later in life when a friend forced a paintbrush into his hands and said, "You need to do this!" Since then Glenn has been diligently working on creating his own brand of beautifully painted images. Using acrylic paints on wooden panels, he adds in elements and influential symbols of his past and present to each piece. Beyond the aesthetics of his artwork, Glenn brings an overwhelming sense of passion to his paintings. Touching on themes of love, death, conflict, and duality, Glenn's art tells stories of strength and hope through emotion and sentiment with his sensual beauties and signature hummingbirds.

Her Fatal Fascination, 2011. Acrylic on wood, 16" x 20" (41 x 51 cm).

The Captain, 2010. Acrylic on wood, 18" x 24" (46 x 60 cm).

The Copilot, 2010. Acrylic on wood, 16" x 20" (41 x 51 cm).

Some Call It an Obsession, 2010. Acrylic on wood, 18" x 24" (46 x 60 cm).

Craig "Skibs" Barker
California

Craig "Skibs" Barker likes legs. This Southern Californian artist grew up during the early '80s in the midst of both the punk rock and surfing culture explosions. These influences soon inspired his own fine art. With a healthy dose of punk flyers, album covers, and surfing magazines buzzing through his head as a youth, Barker began making flyers and t-shirts for his friends and his own punk bands. Fast-forward to today: Barker's most recent paintings infuse his long-standing love for painting and rendering the human female figure with his punk-fueled graphic design. Mixing different approaches, techniques, and mediums, he explores a sense of nostalgia, memory, personal history, and appreciation for the female form. Combining elements of pop culture, literary censorship, and a positive mental attitude, he creates layered scenes of voyeuristic mischief. Barker's work explores the junctions between past and present, memory and imagination, fantasy and reality, while creating a dialog between image and viewer. More recently, he has been making spatially extended versions of these mixed-media creations via three dimensional assemblage pieces, and large scale gallery installations.

With You, 2010. Oil and mixed media on wood, 7.5" x 8.5" (19 x 22 cm).

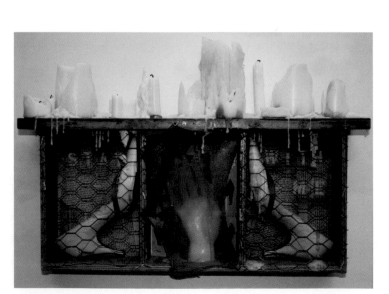

Leave a Trail for Me, 2011. Mixed-media assemblage, 24" x 17" x 8", (61 x 43 x 20 cm).

Mis-Shapen Chaos from Well Seeking Forms, 2011. Oil and mixed media on wood panel with attached shoes, 48" x 72" (123 x 183 cm).

Your Eyes Are Bright Enough, 2009. Oil and mixed media on wood, 10.75" x 13.25 (27 x 34 cm).

Gigi Bio
New York

Gigi Bio's view of the world is a product of the past colliding with the present. She is deeply inspired by culture, bustling streets, speeding traffic, and buildings being torn down and built back up in an instant. She aims to expose the emotional side of the city streets, pushing the final image to abstraction and juxtaposing a new view of the world. She uses the organic, stylized lines seen in graffiti, as an inspiration to drive the flow and mass layering in her work. Her vision resembles a writer's tag, full of life and organic movement. In her eyes, graffiti exists not as an art form, but it exists all around us in reflections, shadows, and buildings. Bio's work is a reflection of life in the streets; each piece represents a world full of ambition, energy, movement, and the re-creation of the world through multiple perspectives captured in various time frames. She encourages the viewer to fully experience the environment by creating a sense of extreme awareness of the world, to appreciate beauty in the mundane, and find order in chaos. Bio's artwork is greatly inspired by the world, but hidden between the layers is a narrative of life, beauty, and transformation.

Thunder Wolf, 2011. Digital photo collage, glicee print on canvas, 36" x 36" (91 x 91 cm).

CAM, 2009. Digital photo collage, glicee print on canvas, 36" x 36" (91 x 91 cm).

Year of the Rabbit, 2011. Digital photo collage, glicee print on canvas, 36" x 36" (91 x 91 cm).

Year of the Ox, 2009. Digital photo collage, glicee print on canvas, 36" x 36" (91 x 91 cm).

Kelly Castillo
California

Kelly Castillo is an artist intertwined in the underground emerging artist scene in Southern California. Not only an urban contemporary artist, she is also a gallery owner, an arts commissioner for the City of Anaheim and the owner of the Anaheim chapter of Dr. Sketchy's Anti-Art School. Castillo made her professional debut as an artist in 2009 and has since been featured in galleries throughout Southern California and on the East Coast. Her involvement with Dr. Sketchy's Anti-Art School is evident in her work. Mainly focusing on portraiture, she uses bold lines to create an illustrative quality in her work using modern media techniques like spray paint, marker, and acrylic paint. Bold color and design juxtaposed with vintage subjects lends itself to a multidimensional audience in love with the old and inspired by the new.

Renaissance Reduxxx: Poux Deux, 2010.
Acrylic paint and pen, 12" x 24" (31 x 60 cm).

Renaissance Reduxxx: Destruction, 2010.
Acrylic paint and pen, 36" x 36" (91 x 91 cm).

Renaissance Reduxxx: Pretension, 2010.
Acrylic paint and pen, 36" x 36" (91 x 91 cm).

Renaissance Reduxxx Series, 2010. Acrylic paint and pen, 12" x 36" (31 x 91 cm).

Paul Chatem
California

Paul Chatem was born in 1974 in Bellevue, Washington, but grew up in La Crescenta on the outskirts of Los Angeles, California. He spent most of his time hunting snakes and scorpions in the Tujunga Wash, exploring the ruins of forgotten ranches, shantytowns, and asylums, and ducking punches at punk shows with his friends. Growing up in an environment where nature, history, and the impoverished were constantly being pushed aside to make room for golf courses and mini-malls, Paul has developed a keen talent for representing the rift between rich and poor, the working man and the boss man, in his surreal, often nightmarish, narrative paintings. In recent years, Paul has been using his carpentry skills to develop new and intriguing pieces that invite the gallery patron to interact with his work. By turning a crank which moves layers of wooden gears, the viewer has the opportunity to change the composition and drive the action of the narrative without the traditional barriers between art and the individual. Paul is currently hiding out in the fog-bound Sierra Foothills with his tortoises, the mud, and the bugs.

Better Start Gettin' Square, 2011. Acrylic on wood, 24" x 24" (60 x 60 cm).

Amarillo Bastard Wine, 2007. Acrylic on wood, 24" x 40" (60 x 102 cm).

The Sidestepper Really Steps in It, 2011. Acrylic on wood, 62" x 46" (158 x 117 cm).

Luke Chueh

California

Born in Philadelphia, but raised in Fresno, Luke Chueh (pronounced CHU) studied graphic design at California Polytechnic State University, San Luis Obipso, where he earned a BS in Art & Design (Graphic Design concentration). In 2003, Chueh moved to Los Angeles to further pursue a career in design. However, a lack of employment opportunities left him resorting to painting as a way to keep busy (a hobby he picked up while attending Cal Poly). He got his start when the Los Angeles underground art show, Cannibal Flower, invited him to show at their monthly events. Since then, Chueh has quickly worked his way up the ranks of the LA art scene, establishing himself as an artist not to be ignored. Employing minimal color schemes, simple animal characters, and a seemingly endless list of ill-fated situations, Chueh stylistically balances cute with brute, walking the fine line between comedy and tragedy. Chueh's work has been featured in galleries around the world, and some of his paintings have also been reinterpreted into vinyl toys.

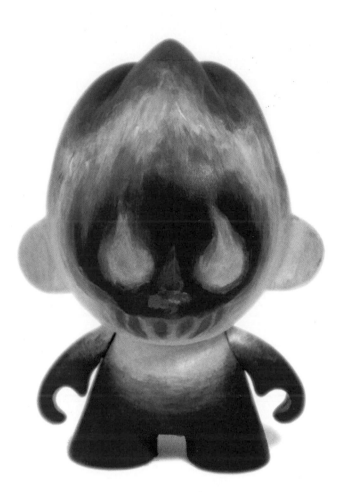

Foomi on Fire, 2011. Acrylic on Munny World Foomi, approx. 6" (15 cm).

Army of Snipers Woebots + Luke Chueh, Dueling Bear Poster (never produced), 2011. 18" x 24" (46 x 60 cm).

Crotch Talk, 2011. Acrylic and ink on paper, 9" x 12" (23 x 31 cm).

LUKE

The Fighter, 2011. Acrylic and ink on paper, 6" x 8" (15 x 20 cm).

David Chung

California

David Chung, aka The Chung!!, definitely has his own unique sense of humor. To the naked eye, his work might suggest that he has the mentality of a fifth grader, and a good pee or poop joke would probably send him into a laughing fit that would cause Charley Horses in his rib cage. However, behind the toilet humor, The Chung!! is a lot deeper (that's what she said) than his work might portray him to be. The world that fills up his illustrations are usually filled with bright vibrant colors and cute squishy creatures who are in a constant state of turmoil. Using a light hearted and humorous approach to dealing with the daily, yet mostly embarrassing issues that many of us have been through at one point or another in our lives, The Chung!!'s work juxtaposes the obscenely adorable with the adorably obscene in an attempt to get people to lighten up. As a child, David's family moved from city to city and country to country due to his father's job. He spent the earlier part of his childhood in the fast-paced, brightly colored cities found in Hong Kong and Taiwan. He finished the remainder of his childhood in upstate New York and finally graduated from college in the Midwest. Having been exposed to both the hyper neon-filled Asian city life and the beautiful nature-filled life of the Midwest, David uses his past and present experiences as his main source of stylistic inspiration.

The Virgin Shrimp Ramen Noodle Soup, 2010.
Acrylic on canvas, 24" x 30" (60 x 76 cm).

Eff Yeah!!, 2011. Acrylic on canvas, 16" x 20" (41 x 51 cm).

Ridin' Dirty, 2010. Acrylic on canvas, 11" x 14" (28 x 36 cm).

Finger-Crab Helps Gillman Try On Mustaches for His Big Date, 2010. Acrylic on canvas, 16" x 20" (41 x 51 cm).

CUTTHROAT
Texas

CUTTHROAT was born in Houston, Texas. His family moved to Atlanta, Georgia, for a few years, then they relocated to Mexico. His early years were spent in Rio Verde, San Luis Potosi. There, in the dusty playground of a private school, he tried to enamor his elementary sweetheart with elaborate colorings of his favorite Disney characters. As a teenager, his family returned to Houston, where he, like most boys from the neighborhood, attached himself to a street gang which quickly assigned him the group's "official tagger." The rush of illegal graffiti fueled his craving for more paint assaults on the streets. He delved into the hip-hop lifestyle and sharpened his skill using the East End and the train yards as a canvas. Now, years later, CUTTHROAT's art has become a widespread in-your-face campaign fusing striking images and a monochromatic palette to invoke politically charged emotions and cultural embracement.

Subcomandante Marcos, 2009. Acrylic on canvas, 30" x 40" (76 x 102 cm).

Emiliano Zapata, 2009. Acrylic on canvas, 30" x 40" (76 x 102 cm).

Frida Kahlo, 2009. Acrylic on canvas, 30" x 40" (76 x 102 cm).

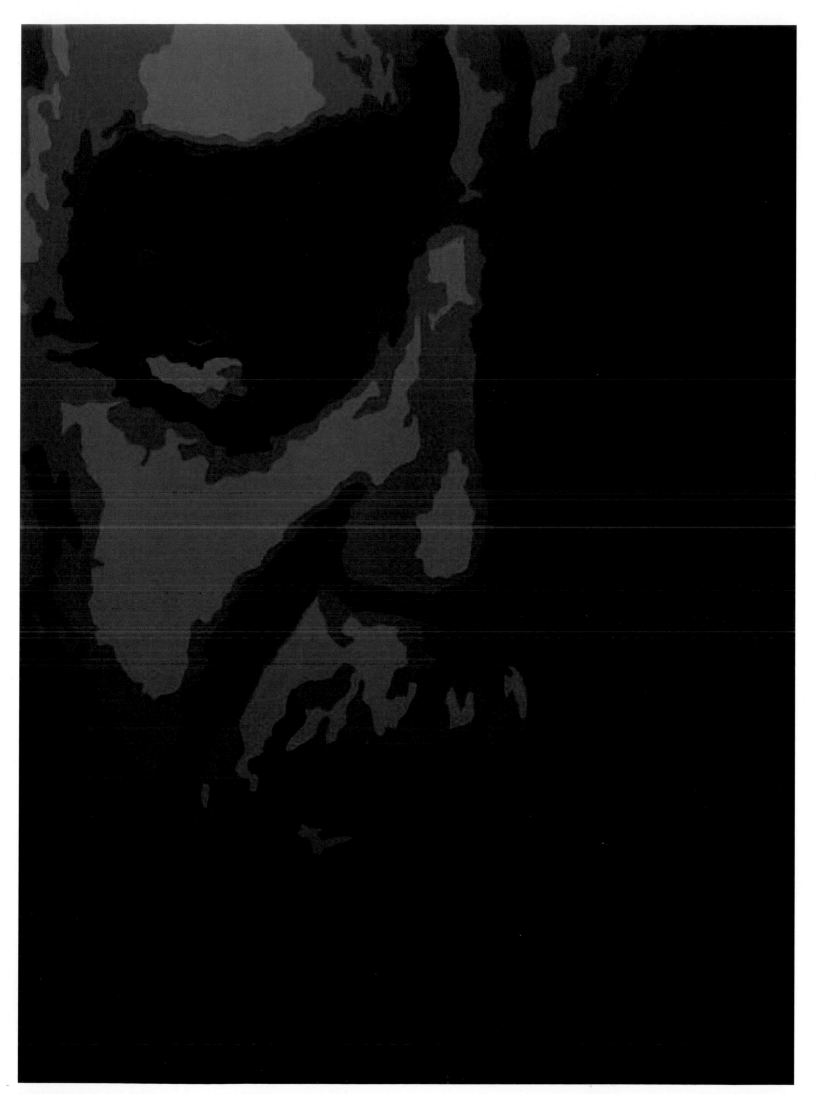

Gabriel Garcia Marquez, 2009. Acrylic on canvas, 30" x 40" (76 x 102 cm).

34

Joey D.
Chicago

Disguised as a corporate douche bag during the day, Joey D., a Chicago native, pushes buttons all day making pictures animate with his magic pen. He secretly escapes into his world of imaginary friends and other made-up things whenever he can. The distorted figures, with their stripe colored underwear and their stick-on noses, are the norm in his universe. Growing up he watched a lot of cartoons, old sitcoms, and played lots of video games. Reading comic books and eating tons of junk food has also messed up his brain. His favorite things include garage sales, thrift stores, dumpster diving, traveling the world, being with family, and most of all, spending time with his wife, Yum Yums, and their new baby.

Windy City Roller, 2009. Acrylic on wood cut out, 14" x 28" (36 x 72 cm).

Please Stand By, 2010. Ballpoint pen and digital photography, 10" x 14" (25 x 36 cm).

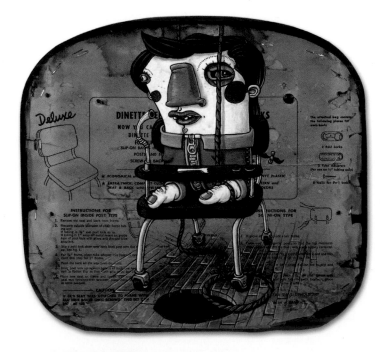

Deluxe Dinette Chair, 2008. Acrylic on chair bottom, 16" x 16" (41 x 41 cm).

The Last Unicorn, 2010. Acrylic on wood tabletop, 18" x 18" (46 x 46 cm).

James "JIMBOT" Demski
Wisconsin

James "JIMBOT" Demski lives in Milwaukee, Wisconsin, with his wife, his daughter, his two crazy dogs, and possibly a captive robot he keeps in his basement. After graduating from art school, James began re-programming his over-schooled brain, and took work as a freelance artist... he has been doing it ever since. His work can be found on clothing, in advertising, magazines, and galleries. Recently, he has found himself being published in the likes of *Juxtapoz Art & Culture Magazine*, *Bluecanvas Magazine*, *ArtBox Magazine*, *ColorInk Book*; creating clothing designs for Lands' End; being chosen as the winner of the Paul Frank 2010 "Art Attack" contest; and more. Besides painting and sculpture, he really enjoys working on his plans for world domination and creating his robot army. Jimbot's influence comes from his childhood and the fears that followed him as he grew up. Cartoons, comics, toys, fun, insecurities, happiness, and anger all intermingle in his work, and he brings all of this together in paintings, drawings, and mixed media. His work usually deals with different emotions and feelings churning inside of him, but more than anything, he likes to have fun with his imagery. Usually, he leaves the interpretation of his work up to the viewer, letting them establish their own ideas of his world, much like how we are left to interpret the real world on our own.

Mine, 2010. 8" x 10" (21 x 25 cm).

Team Beta, 2009. Acrylic on hardboard, 11" x 14" (28 x 36 cm).

The Escape, 2011. Acrylic on canvas, 24" x 24" (61 x 61 cm).

Sea Voyage, 2010. Acrylic on hardboard, 11" x 14" (28 x 36 cm).

Dan Fleres

California

Life and all of its complexities is the source of artistic inspiration for Dan Fleres and what pushes him to take his art to new levels. Through his experimentation's with acrylic, paper, and mixed media on canvas, wood, and found objects, Fleres creates streamlined portraits of mournful yet vividly colored characters against skillfully rendered backgrounds. His work is flavored with his subtle yet insightful views of pop culture and society.

Joie de Vivre, 2011. Acrylic on canvas, 18" x 24" (46 x 61 cm).

The Mothmen of Various Earth, 2008.
Acrylic on canvas, 16" x 20" (41 x 51 cm).

Kidstar, 2009. Acrylic on wood, 20" x 24" (51 x 61 cm).

Winter Still Life, 2011. Acrylic on canvas, 11" x 14" (28 x 36 cm).

Blaine Fontana

Oregon

Blaine Fontana currently lives and works in Portland, Oregon. Imbuing his vision with the divine symbolism of religious myths, worldly folklore, and current social dynamics, his works contain a kind of shamanic exploration of meaning that recognizes the totemic quality and power of the image. With extensive experience within the design world, including working as a designer for Felt Bicycles and acting art director for Zero+ Publishing, Fontana's work displays a virtuosic understanding of sign and simulacra and their role within our contemporary visual culture. Straddling the physical and metaphysical, organic and architectural, painterly and graphic sensibilities, Fontana fuses multiple visual strategies to forge an aesthetic language entirely of his own making.

Fragrance of Mortality, 2010. Acrylic on board, 24" x 24" (61 x 61 cm).

Embrace the Unknown, 2011. Acrylic on canvas, 12" x 12" (31 x 31 cm).

I Dream of "Patience," 2011. Mixed media on paper, 22" x 30" (56 x 76 cm).

Bill's Raven, 2010. Acrylic on board, 18" x 24" (46 x 61 cm).

Graham Franciose

Texas

Relatable and honest, Graham's works are some of the most gentle yet emotionally evocative works ever featured at Art Whino. His imaginative illustrative paintings are small in size and big on emotion, each depicting its own little narrative, often dreamily reminiscent, reaching deep into the human condition and showing us all little pieces of ourselves along the way. "A lot of my work deals with the quiet moments in a story, between the excitement and action, where characters deal with internal conflicts, doubt, loneliness, wonder, apprehension. My work often comes across as sad and melancholy, but there is always a sense of hope that I am trying to portray." After growing up skateboarding and reading comics in rural Massachusetts, Graham Franciose graduated with a BFA in illustration from the Hartford Art School in 2005. He has exhibited his work since then across the United States and Europe. His illustrations have been used in album covers, gig posters, and children's books and have been featured in various art publications. When he is not painting he is probably out enjoying the day, rolling some skeeballs, or sucking down some suds with the folks he is lucky enough to call his friends. He is currently working as a freelance illustrator and fine artist out of Austin, Texas.

Looking for Answers in All the Right Places, 2011.
Ink and acrylic on coffee-stained paper, 20" x 16" (51 x 41 cm).

In Hopes of Emerging Anew, 2011.
Oil and ink on birch panel, 18" x 24" (46 x 61 cm).

The Mistress of the Wetlands, 2011.
Ink and acrylic on coffee-stained paper, 11" x 17" (28 x 43 cm).

A Narrow Escape, 2011. Ink and acrylic on coffee-stained paper, 18" x 24" (46 x 61 cm).

Patrick Haemmerlein

California

A native of Kinderhook, New York, Patrick Haemmerlein is a freelance graphic designer and artist living in Los Angeles. After receiving his BFA from The Savannah College of Art and Design in 2000, Patrick took the long road trip cross country and settled down in LA. There he began to obsessively photograph the city and its components. This gradually moved into a new art form as he started to combine and create with the images he was shooting. Reflecting on the issues of the day, Patrick explores themes of nature versus industry and how they can coexist or clash. The images are all designed from photographs that Patrick has taken. The buildings and cityscapes are from Los Angeles, while the animal and farm photos were mostly taken around his hometown area in upstate New York. They are not only a juxtaposition of nature and industry, but a combination of imagery from his two homes—one rural and one urban.

Managing Editor, 2011. Mixed-media collage, 8" x 12" (20 x 31 cm).

Eminent Domain Series, 2010 (L to R): *War of the Roses, Projecting Beyond,* and *Business as Usual.* Mixed-media collage, 12" x 30" (31 x 76 cm) each.

I'll Be Discovered after My Death, 2008. Digital collage, 8" ×10" (20 x 25 cm).

Walt Hall

California

Walt Hall was born and raised on the mean streets of Kilaminjaro. At the age of seven, he stowed away onboard the HMS *McGuillicuty*, whose privateers had sworn a blood oath to seek and destroy the Barbary Pirates. After twelve years at sea, he bid farewell to his comrades and joined up with a series of leftist guerilla movements in the jungles of Peru. Although the liberation front hated to lose his contributions, three years into the struggle he was secretly extracted, via the underground pipeline of Jesuit missions and Chinese yo-yo distribution centers, and given a new secret mission. A mission from the very top. The objective—the elusive double agent Marco. Marco was a worthy adversary indeed, constantly slipping away just when he finally seemed within reach. But in the end he was no match for Walt Hall. Aided by his superior horsemanship and vast knowledge of local Cossak customs, he finally trapped Marco once and for all inside of a creaky church copula somewhere in south west Ukbekistan and promptly turned him over to the turnip police for a lengthy internment on a secluded penal island thirty two minutes northwest of Guam. In his spare time Walt Hall enjoys weaving oversized afghans from the wool of his prized llama, Freddie. He also fancies painting.

In the Morning, 2011. Mixed media on wood, 24" x 48" (61 x 122 cm).

Birthsong for a Forest, 2011. Mixed media on wood, 23" x 24" (58 x 61 cm).

Our Parade, 2010. Mixed media on wood, 22" x 26" (56 x 66 cm).

Brandon Hill
DC

Brandon Hill is a DC-based, Charm City-raised multi-media artist, sculptor, and designer best known for use of a variety of metal and wood materials from aerosol cans to broken skateboards. If art were the movies, Hill's work is definitely the "Spaghetti Western," a cohesive mix trying to be both throwback and avant-garde. Topics of his work are largely based on human ideas and concepts of culture, community, places, or people, mixed with an emphasis on good craftsmanship, and range anywhere from Noam Chomsky to the fictional RoboCop. Hill primarily uses wood, canvas, steel, and resin in his work. As a result, he has a very diverse skill set that produces everything from 2-D painting, wood sculpture, and illustration to apparel. This has resulted in various collaborations with local and national artist and brands; his work has also been featured in such collections as the Reginald F. Lewis Museum in Baltimore, Maryland.

Yellow Wood, 2011. Pine, birch, and lacquer on skate deck, 6" x 33" (15 x 84 cm).

Natural Selection, 2011. Resin, steel, filler, and enamel, 8" (20 cm).

Fish Scale Pumps (Cheeseburger Sushi), 2007–2008. Acrylic, enamel, and pencil on leather, 5" (13 cm).

Chickenville 100 (diptych), 2011. Acrylic, enamel, and pencil on canvas 44" x 60" (112 x 152 cm).

Joe Iurato
New Jersey

Joe's art can be found in both public spaces and in galleries. His stenciling technique, which he describes as "drawing with an X-acto blade," is completely his own, and it's evidenced within the styling of his works. His cuts are proportionate and clean yet painterly and imperfect. His subject matter varies according to his daily inspirations, from large-scale portraits of children recognizing their importance to society and this planet's future to faceless characters that appear at a crossroads somewhere in between victory and defeat to people "floating and drifting" away with elation and self restoration to his more recent textural paintings of ropes and chains, things that Joe finds symbolic of strength and unity, rather than restraint and oppression. Regardless of the subject matter, Joe's adamant about creating socially conscious work that speaks to the times.

Nobody, 2010. Stencil, latex, and acrylic on wood, 60" x 48" (152 x 122 cm).

Restoration of Self, 2011. Mixed media, 24" x 24" (61 x 61 cm).

I'll Take Care of You, 2011. Stencil and spray paint on wood, 48" x 48" (122 x122).

:01

The Raven, 2011. Mixed media, 16" x 20" (41 x 51 cm).

Aaron Jasinski
Washington

Aaron Jasinski's paintings have shown across the United States and Europe. He also illustrates children's books, album covers, and creates electronic music. Aaron grew up in a family of musicians and the love of music is a major influence in his visual art. His paintings often feature musical and nostalgic themes peppered with social commentary and whimsical creatures (think morose hipsters mingling with monkeys in space suits) and utilize a Technicolor palette. Aaron resides near Seattle, Washington, with his wife and four children.

Clarity, 2010. Acrylic on wood panel, 16" x 16" (41 x 41 cm).

Of But Not In, 2009. Acrylic on wood panel, 18" x 24" (46 x 61 cm).

Progress on the Horizon, 2008. Acrylic on canvas, 24" x 36" (61 x 91 cm).

Make Your Own Destiny, 2010. Acrylic on wood panel, 18" x 24" (46 x 61 cm).

JoKa
Pennsylvania

JoKa is a Philadelphia-based painter specializing in hyper-pointillism, using toothpicks as his sole form of paint application. Using collage, he skews and distorts, pushing familiar images into the surreal. He has been exhibiting his work since 2005 across the country as well as internationally, and in national art publications. In true "necessity is the mother of all invention" fashion, his unique method was developed in lieu of learning how to silkscreen. Instead he developed a technique to provide the same desired effect by dotting black over solid color backgrounds. Extrapolating on that practice, he decided to execute more fleshed out and multi-layered pieces of art in an effort to update and showcase an underused and, nowadays, academic form of painting. Using such a regulated and precise technique leaves no inch of surface without extreme care to detail, and the works beg for closer and repeat inspections.

Stunted Growth, 2007. Acrylic on canvas, 16" x 20" (41 x 51 cm).

The Gravity of Perfection, 2009. Acrylic on board, 16" x 20" (41 x 51 cm).

Strung Up in Timelust, 2010. Acrylic on canvas, 12" x 14" (31 x 36 cm).

Billi Kid

New York

The notoriously harmonious Billi Kid is a street artist determined to refine his voice while leaving an indelible mark on the over-saturated urban and cyber landscapes. A life-long doodler, art enthusiast, and design junkie, his work blurs the lines between graffiti, pop culture, iconography, and art. Never too busy to look, feel, and listen, his collaborative works with artist from around the world have been celebrated in both the media and street art community alike. His passion for the streets has led him to curate ground-breaking exhibitions that have helped bridge the gap between the urban landscape and the sterile indoor environment. Take a close look at it, smile at it, tear it, or cover it with something new. From his hand to the streets at large.

Eames Inspiration, 2010. Part of a benefit for Operation Design.

Greed Is Good, 2010. Sticker collage on wood, 36" x 48" (91 x 122 cm).

Pink Rose, 2011. Giclee print, 42" x 72" (107 x 183 cm).

Russell Simmons, 2011. Sticker collage sandwiched under stenciled plexiglass, 24" x 24" (61 x 61 cm).

Caia Koopman

California

From the land of surf and sea, Caia Koopman has emerged as one of pop surrealism's preeminent female artists. With a well-rounded background from her years spent obtaining her BA in fine arts from University of California Santa Cruz, to her time spent in the skateboarding and snowboarding scenes, Caia's environment has both molded and provided an eclectic background that makes her paintings come to life. With her fine detail for beauty, inclinations toward nature, and collective female spirit, Caia has quickly become one of the quintessential artists fully encompassing the elegance, strengths, and vulnerabilities of femininity.

Blue Sugar, 2011. Acrylic on wood, 6" x 6" (15 x 15 cm).

Wound My Heart, 2011. Acrylic on wood, 16" x 20" (41 x 51 cm).

Bunny Dream, 2011. Acrylic on wood, 9" x 12" (23 x 31 cm).

Lost Souls, 2011. Acrylic on canvas, 36" x 48" (91 x 122 cm).

Aaron Kraten
California

Aaron Kraten grew up in southern California. He loved to draw in small sketchbooks. Throughout the 1990s, Aaron had created more than 600 drawings. In 1999, Aaron started experimenting with painting on found objects. The artwork was first being exhibited in small independent stores and coffee shops then eventually was displayed in local galleries and museums. Aaron is currently painting full time and says "these are the best days of my life."

Blindfold, 2010. Mixed media on wood, 18" x 24" (46 x 61 cm).

Sour Sight, 2011. Mixed media on wood, 11" x 14" (28 x 36 cm).

Crimson Clover, 2011. Mixed media on wood, 24" x 24" (61 x 61 cm).

Lost Sky, 2010. Mixed media on wood, 18" x 24" (46 x 61 cm).

LECKOmio
Germany

Born in Lörrach, Germany, LECKOmio grew up in a household where painting was a daily activity—he was exposed to a great deal of creativity from an early age. Painting comics and characters had always been one of his favorite hobbies as a kid, and with the help of a school friend, he was introduced to graffiti. Following that small introduction, LECKOmio became hooked and they started writing together, sneaking out at night to paint the neighborhood walls. After several run-ins with the law, he took a break from painting outside and concentrated on school, which led him to a future of business management. However, as a burgeoning artist, he was not satisfied. LECKOmio continued sketching and painting, and in 2002 began experimenting with stencils, though completely unaware of the well-established stencil movement in street art outside of his own developments. His work has been entirely self-taught, with trial and error being his greatest mentor. Following his move from home to studio, and finally quitting his job in management, LECKOmio and his art have taken off, cultivating his personal style, developing innovative stenciling techniques like transparency, and exhibiting work in galleries all over the world (US, Middle East, Australia, and all over Europe).

Cap, 2010. Stencils on canvas board, 12" x 12" (30 x 30 cm).

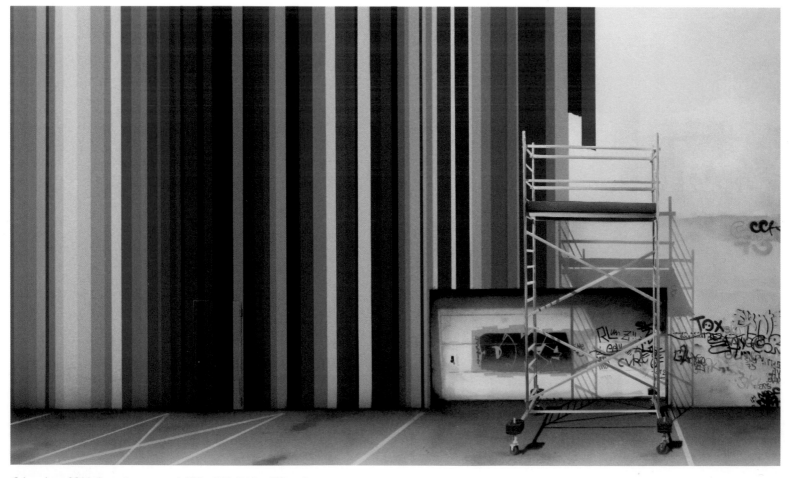

Colourchart, 2011. Stencils on wood, 83" x 39" (210 x 100 cm).

Graffparc, 2010. Stencils on wood, 39" x 39" (100 x 100 cm).

Yosiell Lorenzo
California

Yosiell was introduced to art in his youth during a time when hip-hop and graffiti defined urban culture. Growing up in Bridgeport, Connecticut, he'd hop the train to New York and absorb it all. In the bold lines and bright colors, he saw strength. The writing on the wall seemed to shout: "Look at me! I'm here!" While he admired the intrepid markings of the graffiti writers, Yosiell also found himself looking inward. Inspired by movies like *Labyrinth*, he began to explore the idea of creating his own fictional world through his art with aerosol and acrylic as his escape route. These days, Yosiell has been moving toward a warmer, more subtle and aged palette for his paintings. Each piece is a process of textures and washes. Thematically, he continues to explore issues of sadness and longing, but he works in varying mediums, including sculpting, painting, graphite, ink, mixed media, and digital vector art. He has had a solo show every year since 2008. Additionally, Yosiell makes his presence known in group shows around the country, with events in New York, LA, San Francisco, Chicago, and Miami.

Tristeza, 2010. Mixed media on wood, 12" x 12" (31 x 31 cm).

The Magician Card, 2011. Mixed media on wood, 9" x 12" (23 x 31 cm).

Sickling, Jr., 2010. Mixed media on wood, 12" x 24" (31 x 61 cm).

White Horseman of the Apocalypse, 2011. Mixed media on canvas, 16" x 20" (41 x 51 cm).

Justin Lovato
California

Justin Lovato is a working painter from Sacramento. He currently resides in Berkeley, California. He creates dreamlike, ethereal landscapes that reflect his thoughts on nature and our relation to it, human belief systems, the psycho-political-control system, multidimensional concepts, and esoteric symbolism.

Celestial Ox, 2011. Mixed media, 30" x 25" (76 x 64 cm).

Alchemize that Shit, Dude, 2011. Mixed media, 11" x 14" (28 x 36 cm).

Certain Doom, 2011. Mixed media, 11" x 14" (28 x 36 cm).

Many Ways to Skin a Buck, 2011. Mixed media, 25" x 30" (64 x 76 cm).

Dave Lowell

Texas

Dave uses a combination of multi-layer stencils and freehand aerosol work. His themes range from sexy to urban to country to comedic.... The use of reclaimed and found objects in his art pulls from the environment and the aesthetic of early work only found outdoors. The name "Anomi" is an old name used for street pieces that reappears often in his work. He earned his B.A. studying design at Texas State University and currently resides in Austin, Texas with his wife and two cats.

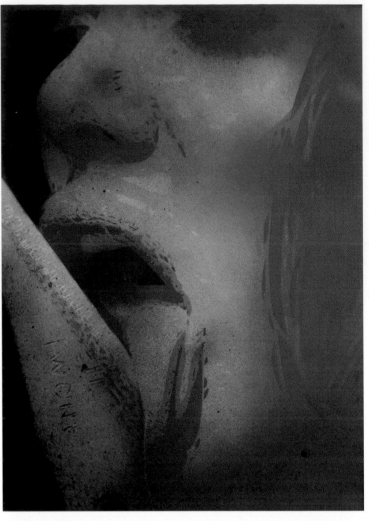

Treats Roja, 2011. Stencil and freehand aerosol, 15" x 20" (38 x 51 cm).

So Hot Right Now, 2010. Stencil and freehand aerosol, 20" x 26" (51 x 66).

Deer Head, For the Home, 2011. Stencil and freehand aerosol, 22" x 28" (56 x 71 cm).

Not What You Wanted? (Boy), 2010. Stencil and freehand aerosol, 19" x 27" (48 x 69 cm).

Jim Mahfood
California

Jim Mahfood, aka Food One, is a freelance artist working professionally in the fields of illustration, advertising, comic books, murals, fine art, animation, live art in nightclubs, and custom body-painting. He has worked for every major comic book company, and his illustrations have appeared in such publications as *Playboy*, *Spin*, *Spectrum Illustration Annual*, *Star Wars Gamer*, *URB*, the *Hollywood Reporter*, *BPM*, the *Phoenix New Times*, *Mad Magazine*, *Heavy Metal*, and more. Highlights of his career include illustrating director Kevin Smith's *Clerks* comics, handling the art chores on the entire ad campaign for Colt 45 malt liquor in 2007-08, painting the murals on Comedy Central's *Sarah Silverman Show*, illustrating the *Kickpuncher* comic book that was included in the Season 1 DVD of NBC's hit show, *Community*, illustrating and art directing reggae legend Ziggy Marley's *MarijuanaMan* project, and providing custom car art for Nissan's new Juke Artist Series. His current project is illustrating the new *Tank Girl* graphic novel, due out in 2012.

Segovia & the Swordfish, 2011. Mixed media, 8.5" x 11" (22 x 28 cm).

Hang Up Your Hang-Ups, 2011. Pen and ink, 9" x 11" (23 x 28 cm).

Pop Life, 2010. Mixed media, 8" x 11" (20 x 28 cm).

Mice Blind (Three), 2011. Mixed media, 9" × 11" (23 × 28 cm).

Nick Morris

Australia

In the beginning—I was a graphic designer. As a graphic designer, I felt that everything I created had to be clean and perfect. As an artist I embrace living on the edge of chaos, bringing it together through balance and color. This I achieve through creating, stuffing around in an art studio, and making things up as I go. I love screen-printing, with its instant gratification and unexpected results. You have no idea what it will look like until you lift up the screen. I work with acrylics, collage, and screen prints, using images from post-war popular culture, Australiana, and my own photographs. Acrylic because it's so quick to work with and if what you have done doesn't work, you can go straight back over the top of it, building texture as you go. Because of this, deep layering is probably the most dominant pattern that emerges in my work. I love the idea that there is so much more to be discovered in a piece than what the eye initially sees. I am satisfied with a piece when the layering of the subject matter, the balance and the color work collaboratively, bringing the piece together —as a composer brings random notes together to produce a melody or harmony.

5 O'Clock, 2011. Acrylic screen print on canvas, 27" x 27" (69 x 69 cm).

Red Blue Target, 2011.
Acrylic screen print on canvas, 45" x 45" (114 x 114 cm).

Love Target 3, 2011.
Acrylic screen print on canvas, 11" x 24" (28 x 61 cm).

Build a House, 2011. Acrylic screen print on canvas, 55" x 40" (140 x 102 cm).

Mr. Christopher

Kansas

Born on the mean streets of Wichita, Kansas, Mr. Christopher had to learn to hustle at a very young age. Art was a game of survival and necessity. On many occasions, he would draw pictures of superheroes on the back of notebooks in trade for other kid's lunches. At the height of Christopher's hustle game, he was earning 5 or 6 sandwiches a week. But then it all came to an abrupt end at the age of 11, when he had a sudden spiritual crisis. He swore he would never draw or paint again. All that changed when at the age of 17, Mr. Christopher discovered graffiti. That culture made him realize that you should produce art not for sandwiches, but for the sake of creating. Everything he creates is for the sake of creating. He doesn't produce his work for any kind of monetary gain, or sandwiches. Mr. Christopher paints because that is what he feels he was put on this earth to do.

Urban Outfitters, 2011. Acrylic and enamel on spray can, 4" x 8" (10 x 20 cm).

Straight Up Wholesome, 2008. Acrylic and spray paint on wood panel, 12" x 24" (31 x 61 cm).

Saint Newton, 2011. Acrylic and gold leaf on wood panel, 8" x 10" (20 x 25 cm).

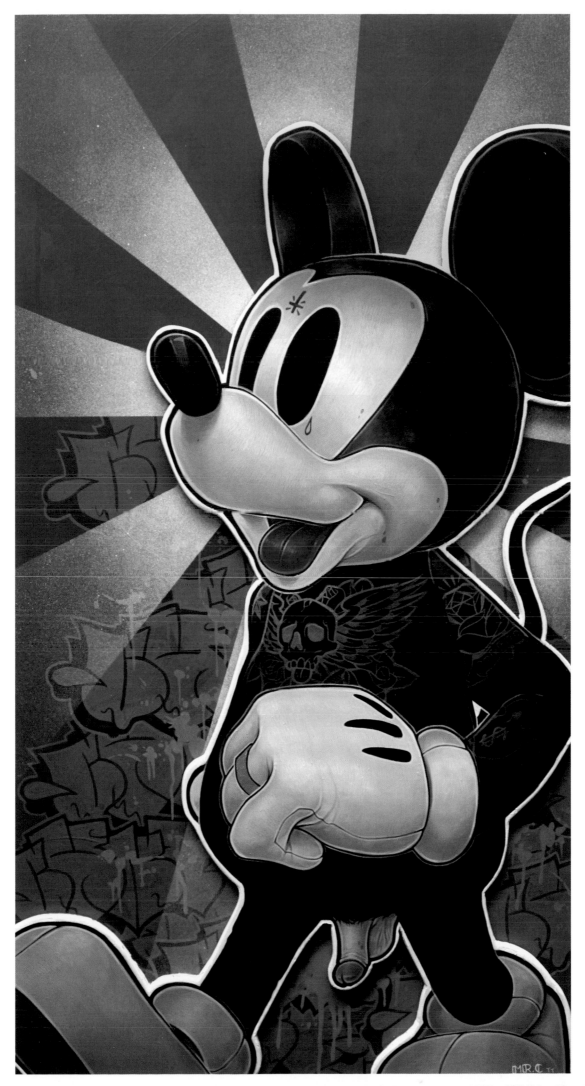

If We Ain't Busy Fuckin', Then I Am Fuckin' Busy, 2011. Acrylic, spray paint, and gold leaf on wood panel, 12" x 23" (31 x 58 cm).

Sylvia O
New York

New York native SYLVIA O has been heavily active in the alternative art scene since 2002. Her imagery uses the female figure as a means to expose the objectification of women, focusing on the often-discarded essence and toy-like portrayal of women displaying an unfiltered obscurity of reality and what "beauty" truly is. Herein lies the grotesque, where society's obsession with beauty creates an unobtainable ideal, often leading to the mutilation of identity. The beautifully grotesque explores the many ways to visually describe what many women endure emotionally, physically, and spiritually, always using symbols of femininity through color, playful, and flirty expressions as well as her signature imagery of floating breasts—all the while solidifying her belief that the beautiful and the grotesque exist as one entity and not as opposites.

Hallow, 2010. Acrylic ink on paper, 13" framed (33 cm).

Carmen, 2010. Acrylic and pencil on archival paper, 8" x 10" (20 x 25 cm).

Red Ribbon #4, 2010. Acrylic ink on canvas, 30" x 30" (76 x 76 cm).

Natalia, 2009. Pencil, ink, and acrylic on paper, 9" x 12" (23 x 31 cm).

Emma Overman

Indiana

Emma Overman was born in Sete Lagoas, Brazil, and raised in a small town in Tennessee. Being equal parts reclusive and escapist, Emma spent her early formative years retreating into books and records. It is largely a lingering appreciation for children's literature and imagery that inspires her work today. She graduated from Hanover College in 1997 and completed the Post Baccalaureate Program at Maryland Institute College of Art a year later. Creating art full time since 2000, Emma has illustrated a few picture books, designed posters for area events, and won two international illustration competitions. These days she spends most of her time on her own independent projects and showing her paintings nationwide. A dominant theme that runs through Emma's work is a sense of elegant nostalgia. Children and animals are often used because she feels they have a greater capacity to communicate emotion than adult characters. Emma loves all the curiosities of childhood, the sense of wonder and uncertainty when experiencing something for the first time, and how the world seems to change from year to year. She has an appreciation for anything that is part sweet and part sad, like the frail and fleeting nature of youth. Emma's paintings are inspired by children's literature, stop-motion animation, and the "It's a Small World" ride. She finds greater influence, however, in the most unlikely places and at the most unlikely moments.

The Pale Imposter, 2009. Acrylic on birch, 13" x 21" (33 x 53 cm).

Annie and the Hilltop Nibbler, 2010. 40" x 35" (102 x 89 cm).

Pig in the Woods, 2010. Acrylic on birch, 30" x 32" (76 x 81 cm).

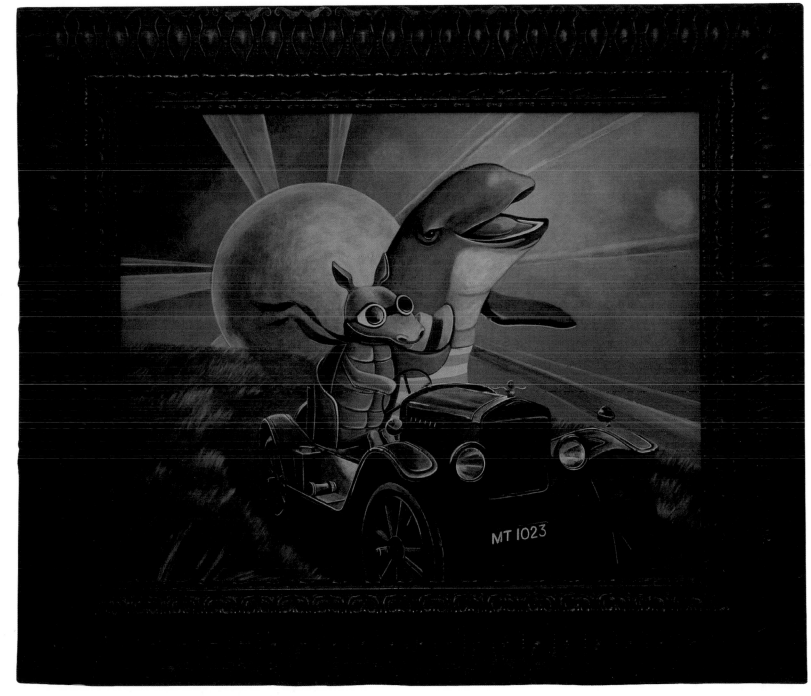

A Journey with a Porpoise, 2011. Acrylic on birch, 26" x 22" (66 x 56 cm).

Charlie Owens

Georgia

Born and raised in Knoxville, Tennessee, artist Charlie Owens moved to Atlanta, Georgia, at the age of 18 to pursue a degree in graphic arts. During his years as a freelance graphic designer, Owens began developing a unique mixed-media style of art that combines his love of urban decay street art, design, and iconic illustration. His gritty design and use of multiple mediums combine to create compelling and distinctive work that has been praised for its stylized female forms and complexity. Owens combines a variety of techniques to create deep texture and interest in his work, including freehand and vector illustration, stenciling, painting, and screen printing. From over-sized installations to poster art, Owens' pursuit of hands-on fine-art craftsmanship and edgy graphic design has combined to produce an amazing catalog of work.

Outlaw, 2009. Mixed media, 48" x 48" (122 x 122 cm).

Right Through You, 2011. Mixed media, 69" x 92" (175 x 234 cm).

Black and White Collection, 2010. Mixed media, 45" x 60" (114 x 152 cm).

Paint It Cherry Red, 2011. Mixed media, 69" x 92" (175 x 234 cm).

Tony Philippou
New York

Tony Philippou's work centers on the juxtaposition of conflicting stereotypes—to create a sense of harmony in a world that shouldn't be possible. His body of paintings is based on figurative forms of iconic personalities that are then tightly rendered in very loose or controlled environments. A blend of art nouveau, figurative, abstract, and surrealist approaches are fused for a more dynamic composition. Cartoons, graffiti, and illustration were at the beginning of his artistic influences. Personal inspiration came from the likes of artists such as Todd Mcfarlane, Jim Lee, Simon Bisley, John Singer Sargent, N.C. Wyeth, Dali, Klimt, and Egon Schiele to name a few. His attraction to draftsmanship combined with random elements of design, color, and fluidity has played a major role in his artistic direction.

Lelantos, 2010. Oil on board, 11" x 14" (28 x 36 cm).

Jeezus Piece Keeping It Mad Real, 2008.
Oil on wood, 16" x 20" (41 x 51 cm).

Judas Piece King Serpentine, 2008. Oil on wood, 11" x 15" (28 x 38 cm).

Mary in BronxZooLand, 2009. Oil on wood, 18" x 24" (46 x 61 cm).

Melanie Pruitt
Colorado

Rural southwestern Nebraska is where Melanie Pruitt was born and raised. She completed a Bachelor of Fine Arts degree from Fort Hays State University. Denver, Colorado, is now her home. Melanie finds solace in studying the beauty of human history. The details of its emotional complexity to the organic patterns of the Rocky Mountains that surround her inspire an obsessive love of line, form, and movement. These intricacies translate both realistically and abstractly into her creative process.

Amanda, 2009. Ink on paper, 18" x 24" (46 x 61 cm).

It's Just Skin, 2011. Ink on paper, 16" x 20" (41 x 51 cm).

She Liked to Keep Herself Clean, 2011. Ink on paper, 24" x 36" (61 x 91 cm).

A Cloud of Ravens, 2010. Ink on paper, 12" x 24" (31 x 61 cm).

Richard Salcido
California

Richard Salcido's work encompasses the process of exhibition development by creating an "exhibition-worthy" piece under a daily time constraint from inception to completion, and embracing the idiosyncratic qualities that unfinished pieces may include. He states that "on certain days some things come together and on other days everything seems to fall apart," but accepts each as it comes. He rejoices both in success and in failure, and finding a balance between what an artist is expected to put into creating a final piece, and what actually results. Though he often wonders why he paints everyday, given he is often left with disappointment, he believes that "there is a beauty in it, because there is a beauty in failing." Drawing from an early influence of comic books and graffiti, his work features figurative, still life, and typographic elements juxtaposed with mixed media and deconstructionist appeal, which highlights the various layers of the compositional process that he strives to exemplify within his work.

Straight Ahead, 2011. Acrylic on wood panel, 8" x 10" (20 x 25 cm).

White Collar. Acrylic on wood panel, 16" x 20" (41 x 51 cm).

Drunken Angel, 2010. Acrylic on wood panel, 16" x 20" (41 x 51 cm).

My World is Grey, 2011. Acrylic on wood panel, 18" x 12" (46 x 31 cm).

SCOTCH!

Texas

SCOTCH! began his artistic stencil career in 2005 by experimenting with self-taught techniques and learning from his then roommate. Best known for the crotch grabbing storm trooper, his first show was a major success, leading to recognition by the *San Antonio Current*, the city's leading cultural publication, as the Best Anonymous Public Artist in both 2005 and 2006. In 2007, *Juxtapoz Art & Culture Magazine* featured SCOTCH! for his triumphant coordination of a public art installation, Uniting Artists through Crime. The artists combined efforts to cover an entire building in their work. Galleries around the world are catching wind of SCOTCH!'s achievements. Besides art shows, he started a line of t-shirts for the German company 500godz which has taken off since its 2009 inception. It would seem that intelligent, artistic, well-made, hilarious shirts are in high demand. SCOTCH! is happy to fulfill this need. SCOTCH! continues to work on new techniques and ideas towards street art and the evolution of his canvas—all further expanding the number of galleries happily welcoming his work.

Lord Vader, 2007. Stencil and aerosol on canvas; framed, 16" x 20" (41 x 51 cm).

Transportation: Truck, 2011. Stencil and aerosol on wood, 17" x 24" (43 x 61 cm).

Wild Style, 2009. Stencil and aerosol on wood, 18" x 26" (46 x 66 cm).

Jump, 2010. Stencil and aerosol on wood, 18" x 26" (46 x 66 cm).

Scribe

Missouri

Donald Ross, also known as "Scribe," is 36 years old and currently lives in Kansas City, Missouri, in the United States. The animated, public murals by Scribe are readily recognizable in Midtown Kansas City and throughout different parts of the United States, Canada, and down into Mexico, where he has both painted murals and had gallery shows. Scribe incorporates a menagerie of animal characters developed over many years representing a particular, self-referential trait that he inserts in various scenarios. Scribe intersperses personal iconography, biblical and fairytale references, and animation and metaphor in works intended as contemporary parables for public audiences, hence the use of his artist name and persona. Through accessible idiom and image, Scribe incorporates humor and play in the conveyance of serious messages regarding personal integrity, attainment of knowledge, and adventure.

Crashing Down Again, 2011. Acrylics, ink, color pencil, and spray paint, 18" x 24" (46 x 61 cm).

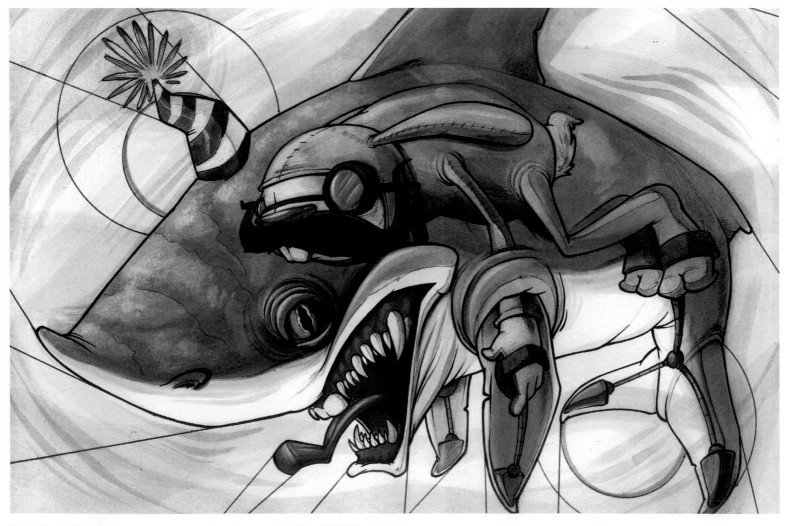

Party Shark, 2011. Acrylics, ink, color pencil, and spray paint, 9" x 12" (23 x 31 cm).

Pastback, 2011. Acrylics, ink, color pencil, and spray paint, 18" x 24" (46 x 61 cm).

Chris Sheridan
Washington

Chris Sheridan grew up on Cape Cod, but after years of moving around the country, he now calls the Pacific Northwest home. Along the way, he received his BFA from the Ringling College of Art and Design in Sarasota, Florida, and his MFA from The Academy of Art University in San Francisco, California. Always game for a good story, for the past few years Chris has been studying (almost obsessively) the histories, mythology, and lore that have shaped different societies, and he has created a large body of work based on those stories that has shown both nationally and internationally.

Mask Series Study #17, 2011. Oil on wood, 7" x 5" (18 x 13 cm).

The Hipster Madonnas, Parts 1-3: Diana, Mary, Isis (triptych: left to right), 2011. Oil on canvas, 60" x 46" (152 x 117 cm).

Headed West (The Sacrifice of the King), 2011. Oil on canvas, 32" x 54" (81 x 137 cm).

Mary Spring
California

Mary Spring's figures are at once both self-portraits of the present and projections of internal hope for the future. Each representation depicts the panoptic range of mental, emotional, and physical conditions experienced in a mere snapshot of time, enabling the observer to merge silently into the psyche of the artist. From ultimate pleasure to unbearable sadness, each expression communicates the profound casualties of insight. The integration of medium and mechanics with design and spirit lead to the paradoxical enlightenment and anguish portrayed at the moment each stroke is applied. Self-realization emerges from the artist as the feminine heart, the kinesthetic demands of performance and dedication, and the consequential strengths are unveiled in each expression. Pain synthesized into passion. Time united with eternity.

The Sample, 2010. Pencil and acrylic on wood, 12" x 36" (31 x 91 cm).

Chase Me, 2009. Pencil, acrylic, and gold leaf on wood, 12" x 18" (31 x 46 cm).

Escape by Indecision, 2008. Pencil, acrylic, and gold leaf on wood, 12" x 12" (31 x 31 cm).

We Don't Sleep Well, 2008. Pencil, acrylic, and gold leaf on wood, 24" x 48" (61 x 122 cm).

Brendan Tierney

California

Brendan Tierney was born in the magical land of New Jersey in the bicentennial year of 1976. He attended the San Francisco Art Institute for a short but very enjoyable time until his heroin habit demanded his full attention. He spent a decade on the stuff, and wound up in Lompoc Federal Prison for three and a half years after foolishly robbing several banks. Brendan learned how to tattoo in prison, which thankfully kept his sweet, skinny ass unmolested. Since being released, Brendan has become a professional tattoo artist, mural painter, and illustrator. After years of being a source of negativity, he had this naive notion to try and put positive, emotion-provoking images out into the world, in hopes of lifting at least a few spirits out there. He found it to be a real challenge to try and convey love and positivity without things turning into some kind of cheesy Hallmark greeting card. He continues to try and share his belief that even in the face of a completely f'd up, cruel, and corrupt world, love, hope, and beauty are the most real and powerful things we have—how's that for a cheesy Hallmark sentiment?

The End, 2011. Acrylic on wood, 20" x 30" (51 x 76 cm).

Shine Down, 2007. Acrylic on canvas, 72" x 48" (183 x 122 cm).

Purchase Your Demise, 2007. Acrylic on canvas, 72" x 48" (183 x 122 cm).

Standing, 2010. Acrylic on wood, 18" x 24" (46 x 61 cm).

TMNK (aka Nobody)

New York

TMNK, aka The Me Nobody Knows, aka NOBODY, is a New York mixed-media street artist whose paintings offer poignant socio-political observations and commentaries on the people and events of contemporary society. Each creation is a spontaneous, yet cerebral mix of symbols, words, and figures used as devices to leave subtle clues for the viewer to interpret or reinterpret. His work has been compared to Picasso, Keith Haring, Romare Bearden, and of course Basquiat. And while he enjoys the comparisons to these great artists, this "nobody" is quite comfortable articulating a variety of subject matters in his own distinctive voice. TMNK's art was recently featured in both *Vibe Magazine* and *YRB Magazine*, is in the permanent collection of the Fleming Museum in Vermont, and was selected for an exclusive line of t-shirts for apparel manufacturer American Eagle Outfitters. With solo shows in New York, Italy, and Norway, this so-called "nobody" has amassed an international following for his unique brand of intellectual urban contemporary art.

Radio Killer, 2009. Acrylic and enamel, 18" x 24" (46 x 61 cm).

Left Every Voice and Scream, 2010. Acrylic and enamel on canvas, 18" x 24" (46 x 61 cm).

Crucified (G40 Wall Installation), 2010 Acrylic and enamel, 240" x 96" (610 x 244 cm).

Lonely Tears, 2011. Acrylic, enamel, and screen print on canvas, 65" x 84" (165 x 213 cm).

Ruben Ubiera

Florida

Ruben Gerardo Ubiera Gonzalez (born October 19, 1975 in Santo Domingo, Dominican Republic) is a Dominican neo-figurative artist known for his strong use of the line. He has been drawing and painting ever since he had use of reason. Ruben paints and draws in a style considered by many as pop-surrealism, but he prefers to call it urban-pop, since he has lived most of his life in the urban, populated areas and most of his inspiration is derived from the interaction between man and his urban environment. At the age of 15 his family moved to the Bronx, New York, where he was heavily influenced by the graffiti art that surrounded him; something he wouldn't realize until much later in his life. He strives in all his work to capture an essential part of his past, his present, and his subjects through the use of the line and form. His work includes still-life and situational portraiture, but Ruben tends to focus primarily on city landscapes.

The Community, 2011. Installation, acrylic on stacked loose bricks, 18" x 18" x 42" (46 x 46 x 107 cm).

Firestone, Miami, 2011. Acrylic on old used skateboards, 45" x 33" (114 x 84 cm).

Sapien Experiment 2, 2011. Acrylic, graphite, and aerosol on newspaper and found chipboard Size: 90" x 96" (229 x 244 cm).

James Walker
Virginia

James never made a conscious decision to become an artist, it's something he's always done for as long as he can remember. He takes pictures and draws and paints and collages debris and objects as intuitively as possible and has never specialized in anything except making the best art that he can. He believes real artists don't have a choice about making art, it's simply a matter of satisfying an insatiable urgency to create. James is formally trained in photography, self-taught in everything else, and he takes a documentary approach to most everything he does with his art. He has always felt that his most successful pieces are ones that develop as a natural extension of existing. Conceptually, James' work comes from a frantic need to dissect the simulacra of the present moment and to be enveloped as completely as possible in every second of every day...any reoccurring themes are simply a by-product of this artistic process.

I Choose My Company By the Beating of Their Heart, 2010. Mixed-media journal page, 8.5" x 11" (22 x 28 cm).

Constellation, 2011. Encaustic, oil, coffee, collage, 36" x 36" (91 x 91 cm).

Preface, 2010. Mixed media with found objects, 12" x 12" (31 x 31 cm).

Stars and Satellites, 2011. Encaustic, oil, coffee, collage, 36" x 36" (91 x 91 cm).

Casey Weldon
New York

Casey Weldon was born in southern California, where he spent the majority of his life up to his graduation from the Art Center College of Design in Pasadena. After a brief time running his own studio in Las Vegas, Nevada, he relocated to Brooklyn, New York, where he now lives and works as an illustrator and fine artist. By using the iconography of today and yesterday's popular culture, his work aims to awaken a feelings of nostalgia within the viewer, though often along with a sense humor, melancholy, and longing for times lost.

Safe Passage, 2011. Acrylic on wood, 30" x 24" (76 x 61 cm).

Alice Liddell, 2009. Acrylic on watercolor paper, 12" x15" (31 x 38 cm).

Second Hand Rat 2, 2010. Acrylic on wood, 18" x 24" (46 x 61 cm).

Lazy Daze, 2009. Acrylic on wood, 18" x 24" (46 x 61 cm).

Nils Westergard
Virginia

Nils took up stenciling at 13 after being introduced to the world of street art by a friend and has been cutting since then. His intricate stencils evolve with every new piece, and are cut with infinite patience. Growing up around Washington, DC, and interacting with the law himself, Nils' work gradually started to focus on the nature of authority, rebellion, and the figures that represent it. But he also has an affinity for graffiti and through his work shows the contrasts between the image of vandalism and the beauty of the art form. His influences range from a large collection of interests, from history to hip-hop. Nils currently attends VCUarts, majoring in the film program.

Girl, 2009. Spray paint on canvas, 36" x 24" (91 x 61 cm).

Kaleidoscoped, 2009. Spray paint and latex on wood, 96" x 48" (244 x 122 cm).

Plenty More Fish in the Sea, 2010. Spray paint on cardboard, approx. 32" x 24" (81 x 61 cm).

Ursula Xanthe Young
California

Over the past fifteen years, illustrator, painter, and designer Ursula Xanthe Young has become known for her unique flowery urban fairytale illustrations. A graduate of Parsons School of Design (illustration, BFA, New York, 1996), Ursula exhibits frequently in the Bay Area and has sold paintings in New York, London, Singapore, Manila, Hong Kong, and all across the U.S. Ursula finds inspiration in the organic yet urban landscape of San Francisco and its surrounds; the crossed wires, Victorian buildings, and fog-filled horizons are a backdrop to her brightly painted doe-eyed flower girls. She is also highly influenced by her frequent travels to the far-flung reaches of the globe and the variety of colorful characters that she encounters—both real and imagined—along the way.

Never a Swan Shall Sing, 2010. Acrylic on wood, 20" x 20" (51 x 51 cm).

Summers Final Calling, 2010. Acrylic on canvas, 30" x 12" (76 x 31 cm).

Dawn of the Decade, 2010. Acrylic on canvas, 30" x 12" (76 x 31 cm).

Psilo Sukhumvit, 2010. Acrylic on wood, 24" x 48" (61 x 122 cm).

Peter Adamyan
www.peteradamyan.com

Brett Amory
www.brettamory.com

Morten Andersen
www.m-andersen.com

Angry Woebots
www.armyofsnipers.com

Glenn Arthur
www.glennarthurart.com

Craig "Skibs" Barker
www.skibsart.com

Gigi Bio
www.gigibio.com

Kelly Castillo
www.kellycastilloart.com

Paul Chatem
www.paulchatem.com

Luke Chueh
www.lukechueh.com

David Chung
www.thechung.com

CUTTHROAT
www.facebook.com/people/Cutthroat-Art

Joey D.
www.joey-d.com

James "JIMBOT" Demski
www.jimbot.com

Daniel Fleres
www.danielfleres.blogspot.com

Blaine Fontana
www.thefontanastudios.com

Graham Franciose
www.grahamfranciose.com

Patrick Haemmerlein
www.urban1028.com

Walt Hall
www.thesappystudio.com

Brandon Hill
www.TheBabychicken.com

Joe Iurato
www.joeiurato.com

Aaron Jasinski
www.aaronjasinski.com

JoKa
www.JoKa444.com

Billi Kid
www.billikid.com

Caia Koopman
www.caiadesign.com

Aaron Kraten
www.AaronKratenArt.com

LECKOmio
www.stefanwinterle.de

Yosiell Lorenzo
www.yosielllorenzo.com

Justin Lovato
www.justinlovato.com

David Lowell
www.davelowellcreative.com

Jim Mahfood
www.jimmahfood.com

Nick Morris
www.nickmorris.com.au

Mr. Christopher
www.themisterchristopher.com

Sylvia O
www.thebeautifullygrotesque.blogspot.com

Emma Overman
www.emmaoverman.com

Charlie Owens
www.charlieowens.com

Tony Philippou
www.tonyphilippou.com

Melanie Pruitt
www.deadlydaisy.com

Richard Salcido
www.richardsalcido.com

SCOTCH!
www.flickr.com/el_scotcho

Scribe
www.scribeswalk.com

Chris Sheridan
www.sheridanart.com

Mary Spring
www.maryspring.com

Brendan Tierney
www.tierneyart.com

TMNK (aka Nobody)
www.menobodyknows.com/nobodyblog

Ruben Ubiera
www.urbanpopsoul.com

James Walker
www.organicdebris.com

Casey Weldon
www.caseyweldon.com

Nils Westergard
www.nilswestergard.com

Ursula Xanthe Young
www.ursulayoung.com